CANADA'S CAPITAL CITIES

Grade 4-6

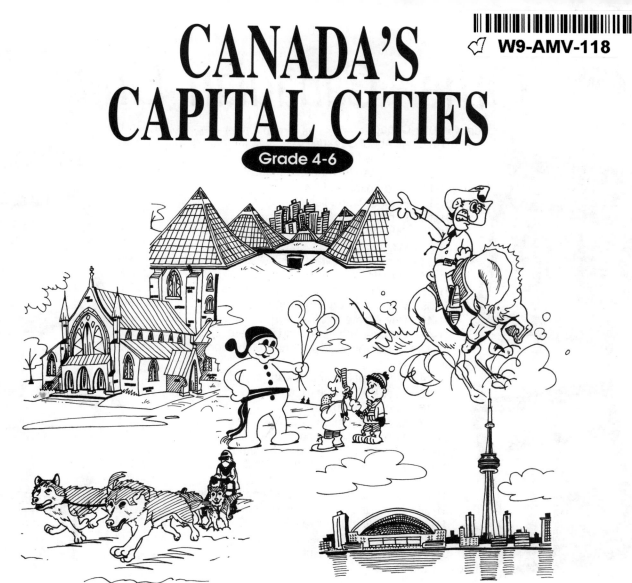

About This Book

Study each of Canada's capital cities. Learn about their land size, population, location, historical and cultural landmarks. Activities include mapping skills, research, art, math, creative writing, science, reading, language, research. Plus Information Cards and Answer Keys!

Written by: Vi Clarke
Illustrated by: Sean Parkes
Item #J1-33

Original Publication: 1996
Revision: 1999
©1996 S & S Learning Materials

Look For Other Canadian Units

Published by:
S&S Learning Materials
15 Dairy Avenue
Napanee, Ontario
K7R 1M4

All rights reserved.
Printed in Canada.

Distributed in U.S.A. by:
T4T Learning Materials
5 Columba Drive, Suite 175
Niagara Falls, New York
14385

CANADA'S CAPITAL CITIES

Table of Contents

"We acknowledge the financial support of the Government of Canada through the Book Publishing Industry Development Program for our publishing activities."

ISBN 1-55035-409-4

Expectations

1. To familiarize students with the size, location, population and importance of Canada's Capital Cities.

2. To acquaint students with the historical importance of each capital city.

3. To discover a variety of tourist attractions in each city.

4. To learn about famous people who live or lived in each capital city.

Teacher Input Suggestions

1. Set up a learning centre to include maps of the world, Canada, the provinces and territories, as well as atlases, encyclopedias, travel guides, current newspaper articles, magazines such as Canadian Geographic, and other materials relevant to a study of Canada's capital cities.

2. Display provincial and territorial flags, coats of arms, flowers, birds, etc.

3. View films and/or videos that provide a visual insight into the capitals.

4. a) Research Canadian Native totem poles. If possible, visit a local museum to find out how they were made and who made them. Students share their findings with the class in a brief illustrated report.

   b) Make a version of a totem pole using cardboard tubes, styrofoam pieces, wood, paper maché, paints, markers, etc. Display the finished products.

5. Invite a local Native leader to speak to the class about Canada's First Peoples. Perhaps he/she can teach the meaning of place names in particular areas that come from the region's Native people.

6. On a map of Canada, have students put a pin or tack on all the capital cities they have visited. Each student tells about what they saw and did in that particular city. Discuss the many customs and traditions that are unique to the area.

7. Students can make a scrapbook about the city in which they live and perhaps send it to a school in another province or territory so that they can learn about the likenesses and differences around the nation.

8. Explain to students the importance to all Canadians of our National Parks and Historic Sites. Suggest they visit as many Parks and Historic Sites as possible on their next family vacation. Ask them to take notes!

9. Create a classroom version of "Front Page Challenge". Explain the format and have students pretend they are a person, place, or event in Canadian history. Have classmates guess who or what the student represents. Set a time limit to make it more fun!

CANADA'S CAPITAL CITIES

10. Make sure that all students know the words to "O Canada" in both official languages. Sing it every morning.

11. Have students recognize all twelve provincial/territorial flags and other pertinent symbols.

12. Students should be able to create an original board game about Canada, focusing on the capital cities.

13. As a culmination to the unit, have parents organize a "pot luck" dinner honouring Canada's multicultural heritage. Bon appétit!

List of Resources

1. Bender, Lionel. **Canada - People and Places**. Morristown, New Jersey, Silver Burdett Press; © 1988

2. Edwards, Frank B. and Kraulis; J.A. **Ottawa - A Kid's Eye View**. Newburgh, Ontario, Bungaloo Books; © 1993

3. Francis, R.D., Richard Jones and D.B. Smith. **Destinies: Canadian History Since Confederation**. Toronto, Ontario; Holt, Rinehart & Winston; © 1988

4. Hocking, Anthony. **The Yukon and the Northwest Territories**. New York, McGraw-Hill Ryerson; © 1979

5. Law, Kevin. **Canada**. New York, Chelsea House Publishers; © 1990

6. Le Vert, Suzanne. **Let's Discover Canada Series**. New York, Chelsea House Publishers; © 1991

7. Malcolm, Andrew. **The Canadians**. New York, Random House; © 1985

8. Murphy, Wendy and Jack. **Toronto.** Woodbridge, Connecticut, Blackbirch Press; Inc.; © 1992

9. Schemenauer, Elma. **Canada Rainbow Series- Cities.** Agincourt, Ontario; G.L.C. Publishers Ltd.; © 1986

10. Shadbolt, Doris. **The Art of Emily Carr.** Toronto, Ontario; Clarke - Irwin/Douglas and McIntyre; © 1979 (The text may be advanced but students should enjoy looking at reproductions of the artist's works.)

11. Shephard, Jennifer. **Canada**. Chicago, Children's Press; © 1987

12. Smith, P.J. ed. **The Prairie Provinces**. Toronto, Ont., University of Toronto Press; © 1972

13. Statistics Canada. **Canada: A Portrait,** Ottawa, Ontario; Statistic's Canada; © 1991

14. Toner, Ogden. **The Canadians.** New York, Time Life Books; © 1977

15. Wansbrough, M.B. **Great Canadian Lives**. New York, Doubleday; © 1986

16. Woods, Shirley E. **Ottawa: the Capital of Canada**. Toronto, Ontario; Doubleday Canada; © 1980

Canada's Capitals - An Introduction

Canada is the second largest country in the world having a land area of about 9 976 185 km² (3 851 809 sq. miles). There are over 25 million Canadians.

Canada is an independent country. It is part of the British Commonwealth and the British Queen is the Head of State. The Canadian nation is made up of ten provinces and three territories. In 1999, a new territory called Nunavut was created. It is part of the Northwest Territories. Each province has its own provincial government and controls many of its own affairs such as highways and education. Québec, Ontario, Nova Scotia and New Brunswick were the first provinces to join a single Government of Canada in 1867. Within four years, Manitoba and British Columbia also joined and the new Canada stretched from sea to sea. By 1905, Prince Edward Island, Saskatchewan and Alberta were added. In 1949, Newfoundland became the tenth and last province to join the Canadian Confederation. The three territories of Canada are The Yukon Territory, The Northwest Territories and Nunavut. They are largely uninhabited and remain Canada's last true areas of wilderness.

The map which follows shows Canada's ten provinces and three territories, along with their capital cities. The largest province is Québec which covers 1 667 926 km² (643 986 sq. miles). The smallest is Prince Edward Island covering 5 656 km² (2 184 sq. miles). About one third of Canada's population lives in Ontario.

CANADA'S CAPITAL CITIES

St. John's

Capital of Newfoundland and Labrador

One of the oldest cities in North America is St. John's, the capital city, principal port and commercial centre of the province of the island of Newfoundland and mainland Labrador.

St. John's achieved much of its importance because of its geographic position. It is closer to Europe than any other city in North America. It is the place where Marconi, an Italian inventor, received the first ever trans-Atlantic wireless transmission on Signal hill in 1901. In 1919, Captain John Alcock and Lieutenant Arthur Brown flew from St. John's Newfoundland to Clifton, Ireland, completing the first nonstop flight across the Atlantic Ocean. St. John's is where Britain staked its first colony and fought its final battle with France in the Seven Years War. It is the home of North America's first Court of Justice, set up in Trinity in 1615.

Though it is a busy progressive port, St. John's retains many historic buildings and sites. To salute the city's birthday, St. John's celebrates Discovery Day in June. The most popular reminder of the city's past is the St. John's Regatta held in August. Dating from at least 1826, it is considered one of the oldest organized sporting events in North America. The Regatta takes place on a lake called Quidi Vidi.

St. John's became the capital of Newfoundland when it became a province in 1949. Today it has a population of about 95 800. John Cabot, the explorer was probably the first European to visit the area in 1497. He likely named it for St. John the Baptist since he arrived on his feast day. Many explorers and fishermen were drawn here in the 1500's because of the perfectly sheltered harbour and rich fishing waters. St. John's covers 83 sq. km (30 sq. miles) on the Avalon Peninsula at the southern end of the island of Newfoundland.

CANADA'S CAPITAL CITIES

St. John's

Facts and Figures

1. Shade in Newfoundland and Labrador on the map. Label St. John's the capital city.

2. a) Where is St. John's located?
   b) How large is the city in area?

3. The populations of several of Canada's largest cities are listed below. Read the information and answer the questions.

City	Population
St. John's	95 770
Halifax	114 455
Toronto	2 400 000
Montréal	1 017 666
Québec City	167 517
Ottawa	313 987
Winnipeg	616 790
Regina	179 178
Edmonton	616 741
Calgary	710 677

a) Which is the largest city?

b) Which cities have more than 500 000 people?

c) Write the populations of St. John's and Montréal in words.

d) Round each population to the nearest thousand.

4. Why were explorers and fishermen attracted to the area in the 1500's?
5. When did St. John's become the capital of Newfoundland?
6. Draw and colour the provincial flag and coat of arms for Newfoundland. Tell the significance of the symbols.
7. What is the provincial motto?
8. What is the provincial flower?
9. What is the provincial bird?

CANADA'S CAPITAL CITIES

St. John's - Landmarks

Rising 160 metres (525 ft.) above the narrow approach to St. John's Harbour is Signal Hill. In the eighteenth century, Newfoundland was coveted by both England and France for its rich fishery. Because of its strategic location, the area saw many battles between the English and the French for control of Newfoundland and its fisheries. The British defeated the French in 1762 in the last battle between the two countries in North America. Because of its height and position at the mouth of the harbour, the site was also an important communications post. Signal Hill was known in the 18th century as the Lookout, and there residents would watch for flags hoisted on incoming ships and inform harbour pilots and customs officials. In 1901, Marconi received the first wireless signal there. A summer tradition since it was first performed as a centennial celebration in 1967, the Signal Hill Tattoo re-enacts militray exercises performed by the Royal Newfoundland Companies garrisoned at Signal Hill.

Other landmarks and special places to see while visiting St. John's are listed below. Write one or two sentences telling of their significance.

1. *Cape Spear National Historic Site*

2. *Newfoundland Museum*

3. *Newfoundland Freshwater Resource Centre*

4. *Ocean Sciences Centre*

5. *Bowring Park*

6. *Commissariat House*

7. *Witless Bay*

Have you ever visited any of these special attractions? If so, which was your favourite?

Are there other landmarks in St. John's that you would recommend to visitors?

CANADA'S CAPITAL CITIES

Lighthouses

Situated on the easternmost point of North America is Cape Spear National Historic Site, near St John's Newfoundland. It is known for its lighthouse on a rocky cliff 75 metres (245 ft.) above sea level. The 1835 structure is one of Newfoundland's oldest surviving lighthouses. For more than a century (one hundred years) it served as an important approach light to St. John's, eleven kilometres (seven miles) to the north. During World War Two a coastal defense battery at Cape Spear protected St. John's from enemy submarines. The lighthouse has been restored and refurbished to pass on the tradition of lighthousekeeping in the province.

Answer the following questions about lighthouses.

1. What is the purpose of a lighthouse?

2. What are lighthouses built of?

3. Why are lighthouses not as important today as they were before the 1940's?

4. a) About how many lighthouses are used worldwide today?
    b) How many are in the United States?
    c) How many are in Canada?

5. Describe what most lighthouses look like. What are "daymarks"?

6. a) Why do most lighthouses today not need a lighthouse keeper?
    b) What were the duties of a lighthouse keeper?
    c) Lighthouse keepers often lived with their families in or near the lighthouse. Pretend that you live with your family in a lighthouse. Your father is the lighthouse keeper. What do you think life would be like? Would you have to go to school? If not, how else could you get your education?

8

Halifax, Capital of Nova Scotia

Because of the harbour that extends inland 26 km (16 mi.), Halifax, the capital of Nova Scotia, was one of the first English settlements in Canada. It was founded in 1749 by Edward Cornwallis, who recognized the site's potential as a naval and military depot. After the British attained supremacy throughout Canada in 1763, Halifax served as the Atlantic headquarters for the Royal Army and Navy.

Until World War I, Halifax's military character was moderated by a civilian shipbuilding industry, which brought considerable wealth to the port economy. During World Wars One and Two, the city was part of the North American lifeline to war-torn Europe. Halifax still remains the principal naval port on Canada's east coast.

This commercial, administrative and military centre of Atlantic Canada is distinguished by a blend of modern office towers and restored buildings and shops. Many of the city's historic buildings were constructed by order of Prince Edward, Duke of Kent, Halifax's commander in chief from 1794 to 1800. Some of these buildings include St. George's Round Church, Prince's Lodge on Bedford Basin, and Government House. Prince Edward was an extremely punctual man. He ordered the building of the Town Clock on Citadel Hill in 1800. On order to curtail tardiness, the prince had the clock constructed with four faces and placed it where it could be seen everywhere in town. Mariners in Halifax Harbour could check their ship's timepieces by the firing of the noon gun, which has been a daily occurrence for nearly two hundred years.

Today Halifax city has a population of about 114 500 (1991). The economy depends heavily on military bases in the area. Over one hundred manufacturing plants operate in the Halifax area. Food processing and oil refining are two of the city's leading industries.

Halifax has more than fifty public schools. Institutions of higher learning include Dalhousie University, Mount St. Vincent University, St, Mary's University, Nova Scotia College of Art and Design, and the Technical University of Nova Scotia. The Bedford Institute of Oceanography makes Halifax one of the largest centres of ocean study in the world.

All the eyes of the world were on Halifax from July 15 to 17, 1995, when Halifax hosted the G-7 Summit. Nine leaders from around the world met to discuss political and financial matters. Canadian Prime Minister, Jean Chrétien, was host of the three day summit.

Halifax Harbour, the second largest natural harbour in the world, separates Halifax from her twin city, Dartmouth. Two toll bridges, the Angus L. Macdonald and the A. Murray MacKay, span the harbour and a regular passenger ferry service connects the two downtown areas.

 J1-33

CANADA'S CAPITAL CITIES

Halifax - Facts and Figures

1. Shade in the province of Canada. Label Halifax, the capital city.

2. a) When was Halifax founded?
   b) By whom?

3. a) Who was Prince Edward?
   b) Why did he have the Town Clock constructed on Citadel Hill in 1800?

4. What is the population of Halifax?

5. What colleges/universities are located in Halifax?

6. a) What is Halifax's twin city?
   b) What two bridges link the twin cities?

7. What worldly event took place in Halifax in 1995?

8. Draw and colour the flag and coat of arms for the province of Nova Scotia. Tell what the symbols represent.

9. What is the provincial motto?

10. What is the provincial flower?

11. What is the provincial bird?

CANADA'S CAPITAL CITIES

Halifax - Landmarks

In Halifax, you can put together a dinosaur puzzle at the Nova Scotia Museum of Natural History on Summer Street. You can watch a movie of the excavation of an Acadian house and listen to the excitement in the voices of the excavators. You can even walk beneath a life-sized model of a huge whale. On the outside of the museum is a huge lifelike model of a frog made by the artist, David Coldwell. There is a botany galleria as well as other galleries that focus on birds, insects and small and large mammals.

Other places to see while in Halifax are listed below. Write one or two sentences describing the importance of each.

1. *Halifax Citadel National Historic Site*

2. *The Town Clock*

3. *Public Gardens*

4. *Point Pleasant Park*

5. *Maritime Museum of the Atlantic*

6. *Art Gallery of Nova Scotia*

Have you visited any of the above? If so, which is your favourite? Can you recommend other special places for people to visit while in Halifax?

The Halifax Explosion

Thursday, December 6, 1917 dawned bright and clear in Halifax. World War One had brought activity and prosperity to the port. At 7:30 a.m., the French munitions ship "Mont Blanc" left her anchorage outside the Harbour to join a convoy in Bedford Basin preparing to go to Europe; she was loaded heavily with ammunition. At the same time the Norwegian steamer "Imo" set out from the Basin headed to New York. For some reason both vessels steered for the same side of the narrow channel joining Halifax Harbour and Bedford Basin. The ships collided causing a fire that ignited the volatile cargo of the munitions ship. At 9:04 a.m., the ensuing explosion literally blew the "Mont Blanc" to pieces, heaved the "Imo" onto the Dartmouth shore, levelled the north-end of the city, killing more than 2 000 people and injuring 9 000 more. Windows shattered 80 km. (50 mi.) away and the shock wave was even felt in Sydney 432 km (270 mi.) to the north-east. Compounding this disaster a blizzard struck the city the following day dumping 40 cm (16 in.) of snow over the ruins! Relief came from all over the world - the U.S., China and New Zealand in the form of money and goods.

Today reminders of the event - gravestones, artifacts and monuments - mark the city which commemorates "The Halifax Explosion" every year on December 6. A moving exhibit of the Explosion "Halifax Wrecked" can be seen at the Maritime Museum of the Atlantic.

Questions:

1. In what year did The Halifax Explosion take place?

2. Name the two ships involved.

3. What cargo was aboard one of the vessels?

4. Describe in your own words the disaster that shook the city.

5. What was the result?

CANADA'S CAPITAL CITIES

Charlottetown, Capital of Prince Edward Island

Prince Edward Island is situated in the Gulf of St. Lawrence on Canada's east coast. The cresent-shaped island is separated from its neighbouring provinces, Nova Scotia and New Brunswick, by the Northumberland Strait, 9 to 14 km across. Prince Edward Island is Canada's smallest province. The capital and only city is Charlottetown with a population of more than 15 000.

The French had designs on the Charlottetown area as far back as 1720. It was then called Port La Joye. In 1758, after Prince Edward Island surrendered to Britain, the British named it Charlottetown after Queen Charlotte, wife of George III.

In Canadian history, Charlottetown is best remembered as the site of the Charlottetown Conference of 1864. Twenty-three delegates from Upper and Lower Canada (now Ontario and Québec), Nova Scotia, New Brunswick and Prince Edward Island met for five days to consider a political-economic union that resulted in the formation of the Dominion of Canada three years later. The Charlottetown Conference represented the all-important first step in the building of the new Canadian nation, thereby meriting the title "Cradle of Confederation".

Presently Charlottetown is a commercial and educational centre. The city has no polluting, heavy industry. It is the major centre for the Island and has the only commercial airport. Its main exports are agricultural products. Its main imports are petroleum products. Tourism is an important industry of Charlottetown. The major roads of the Island spread outwards from the capital, which is centrally located and easily accessible to all other parts of the province. Two major tourist attractions are the Confederation Centre of the Arts and Province House.

Charlottetown is the home of the University of Prince Edward Island and the Atlantic Veterinary College. Also in Charlottetown is the Holland College Technical Institute, which includes the Atlantic Police Academy.

CANADA'S CAPITAL CITIES

Charlottetown - Facts and Figures

1. Shade in Prince Edward Island on the map. Label Charlottetown, the capital city.

2. a) What important meeting in Charlottetown led to the formation of the Dominion of Canada in 1867?
   b) In what year was this meeting held?
   c) Where did the delegates come from?
   d) What important title did Charlottetown merit as a result of this conference?

3. What are two major tourist attractions in Charlottetown?

4. a) Where would you go in Charlottetown to study to become a veterinarian?
   b) If you wanted to become a member of the police force in Atlantic Canada, where in Charlottetown would you go to study?

5. What is the population of Charlottetown?

6. How did Charlottetown get its name?

7. Draw and colour the flag and coat of arms for P.E.I., Canada's smallest province. Tell what the colours and symbols represent.

8. What is the provincial motto?

9. What is the provincial flower?

10. What is the provincial bird?

CANADA'S CAPITAL CITIES

Charlottetown - Landmarks

One of Canada's most historic buildings is Province House in Charlottetown. The building was constructed in 1847 to serve as the Legislature for the colony of Prince Edward Island and it became the centre of public life on the Island.

One event hosted at Province House changed the course of Canadian history forever. The Charlottetown Conference was held in September, 1864. At this meeting the Fathers of Confederation from Upper and Lower Canada (now Ontario and Québec), New Brunswick, Nova Scotia and Prince Edward Island met to discuss the advantages of a Canadian Union. This led to the signing of the British North American Act in 1867 and Province House became known as the "Birthplace of Confederation". The building was restored to its original appearance in 1974.

Below are listed other places of interest to visit when in Charlottetown. Do some research and write one or two sentences telling why each one is a special attraction.

1. *Confederation Centre of the Arts*

2. *Queen's Square*

3. *St. Dunstan's Basilica*

4. *Beaconsfield*

5. *All Soul's Chapel*

6. *Ardgowan National Historic Park*

Have you visited any of the above places? If so, which ones?

Are there other historic sites in Charlottetown that you have seen?

CANADA'S CAPITAL CITIES

Lucy Maud Montgomery

Charlottetown's most impressive modern building is the Confederation Centre of the Arts which was officially opened by Queen Elizabeth II in 1964. Inside the centre are a memorial hall, a theatre, an art gallery and museum, and a provincial library. Every summer since 1965 the theatre has presented the musical play "Anne of Green Gables" written by Don Harron and Norman Campbell, based on Lucy Maud Montgomery's novel.

Lucy Maud Montgomery (1874 to1942) wrote a story about an innocent, red-haired, freckle-faced orphan named Anne Shirley. Anne won the hearts of an elderly brother and sister who lived on a farm in Prince Edward Island. The story was first published in 1908. This was Maud's first novel and she used the Green Gables House as a setting. Since then the book _Anne of Green Gables_ has been translated into more than four languages and has sold over sixty million copies worldwide. A film and television series have been made of the book.

Even though Lucy Maud Montgomery is best known for the Anne series, she wrote other novels just as enchanting as the Anne series, such as the _Emily series, the Pat series, the Story Girl_ series, as well as other novels that were not part of a series, and an autobiography entitled _The Alpine Path_.

Lucy Maud Montgomery is Prince Edward Island's most famous author. Do some research to find out _the most famous author from your province_. Use the information to write a biographical sketch telling about his/her life and accomplishments. What is his/her most famous published book?

Now _you_ be the author and write a fictional story about a girl or boy living in your area. Think of characteristics that best describe your chosen character, develop an interesting plot, add supporting characters, and finish up with a good ending.

Perhaps your main character will be as delightful and unpredictable as Anne Shirley. Perhaps your efforts will result in a best seller!

CANADA'S CAPITAL CITIES

Fredericton, the Capital of New Brunswick

Fredericton, New Brunswick's lovely elm-shaded capital city, stretches along the banks of the Saint John River. The city is 135 km inland from the Bay of Fundy. In 1848, with a population of only 4 400, Fredericton became a city. Then in 1974 several surrounding communities, Marysville, Devon and Nashwaaksis united with Fredericton and the population rose to 44 000. In 1991, the population was 46 500. The area of the city increased from 60 to 132 sq. km. Fredericton was named after Prince Frederick, son of King George III of England.

Fredericton was at one time a British military headquarters. Traces of this period are in evidence at Officers' Square and Compound, and the sounds of marching feet and shouts of command can still be heard all summer during the changing-of-the-guard, a colourful and daily downtown spectacle. The historic parade square today is a centre for entertainment and activity. The former residence for officers is now a museum.

Fredericton is also an important centre for the arts. Crafts are found everywhere and the New Brunswick Craft School, located on the military compound, is the only post-secondary institute of its kind in Canada. Many widely-acclaimed pewtersmiths live in Fredericton. This capital city is the site of the internationally - renowned Beaverbrook Art Gallery, the most impressive showcase of art in eastern Canada, as well as Christ Church Cathedral, one of the finest examples of Gothic architecture in North America.

The University of New Brunswick is one of North America's oldest colleges; it has interesting buildings on campus including the Provincial Archives, Canada's first astronomical observatory, the Old Arts Building, and the Burden Academy, a restored one room schoolhouse. Next door is St. Thomas University, a small, congenial liberal arts centre.

Fredericton's industries include meat processing, shoe manufacturing and steel fabrication. The major employers are the provincial and federal governments. In 1974, Kings Place opened and it includes business offices and a shopping centre.

Fredericton is governed by a mayor and councillors. Who is today's mayor of Fredericton?

J1-33

CANADA'S CAPITAL CITIES

Fredericton - Facts and Figures

1. Shade in the province of New Brunswick on the map of Canada. Label Fredericton, the capital city.

2. What is the area of Fredericton?

3. What is the city's population?

4. What evidence is there that Fredericton was once an important military centre?

5. Choose words from the reading that mean the same as the following:

   a) historical documents
   b) principal church in a diocese
   c) lavish public show
   d) after high school
   e) known throughout the world
   f) style of buildings
   g) a school for specialized training
   h) building equipped for observation of stars or the weather
   i) pleasant; agreeable
   j) manufacturing

6. Draw and colour the flag and coat of arms for the province of New Brunswick. Tell what the symbols represdent.

7. What is the provincial motto?

8. What is the provincial flower?

9. What is the provincial bird?

         J1-33

CANADA'S CAPITAL CITIES

Fredericton - Landmarks

People who either live in Fredericton or visit it like it not only because it is a pretty, safe and clean capital city, but also because of the many wonderful things to do and sights to see.

The incredibly beautiful Saint John River is a focal point of city life with docking facilities in the heart of downtown Fredericton. The 724 km (450 mile) long river was originally called "oa-lus-tuk" or "goodly river". It was the first route travelled by the Malecites and Micmacs as well as the region's earliest settlers - Acadians, Loyalists, Scots and Danes. It flows through rolling hills, rich forests and rigid gorges on its way to the Bay of Fundy. Each summer the River Jubilee Festival pays tribute to the river.

Listed below are other features that are enjoyed by many. Do some research and write a sentence or two telling why each one is important to Fredericton's history.

1. *Fredericton Lighthouse*
2. *The Playhouse*
3. *New Brunswick Sports Hall of Fame*
4. *Brydone Jack Observatory*
5. *Fredericton City Hall*
6. *Christ Church Cathedral*
7. *School Days Museum*
8. *Guard House and Soldiers' Barracks*

Have you visited any of these sites in Fredericton? Which was your favourite?

Can you list other special attractions that would be worth visiting in Fredericton?

CANADA'S CAPITAL CITIES

Glad "Tide"- ings

On your travels across the province of New Brunswick, one of the top attractions to see would be the Hopewell Rocks. Five-storey high flowerpots have been gouged out of the cliffs by the magnificent force of the Fundy Tides. These tremendous tides are the higest tides ever recorded anywhere. The tide has been measured at 14.8 m (48.6 ft.) - that is the height the water has risen!

A) _Why are the Fundy tides so high?_

Fundy tides are the highest in the world because of the shape and dimensions of the Bay of Fundy. When the tidewater enters the bay at its widest point, it comes in just as it does elsewhere in the world. But the farther it travels the more it changes. The water literally piles up as it moves up the funnel-shaped bay. It is, in effect, squeezed by the ever-narrowing sides and the constant shallowing of the bottom, forcing the water higher up the shore.

The length of the bay is another reason the Fundy Tides are so high. When the low (ebb) tide runs out of the bay, it joins the new incoming high tide, combining forces to make an even higher wave coming in. The combination of wave forces is called resonance. The length and depth of the basin determine its particular rhythm. The water of the Bay of Fundy rocks from one side to the other in time with the water in the Atlantic Ocean.

B) _How do they work?_

How the tides work is rather complex, but it is the pull of the moon that is most dominant. When the moon and the sun are aligned with earth at new and full moons, the combination of tidal forces from the sun and the moon results in tides that are twenty percent higher than normal. These are called spring tides, not for the season of the year but simply meaning "when waters spring up from the sea". When the pull of the sun and moon are at right angles to the earth during the first and third quarters of the moon, the tides are lower and are called neap tides from the Anglo-Saxon word meaning "sparse" or "scanty".

 J1-33

CANADA'S CAPITAL CITIES

Spring tides are the greatest.

Neap tides are smallest.

Follow-up Questions:

1. How do the tides play a role in shipping and fishing in New Brunswick?

2. How do the tides influence the weather?

3. How are the tides instrumental in providing food for the many birds, fish and marine mammals that make the bay at least a temporary home?

4. Dulse is a product harvested at low tide. What is dulse?

5. Are the Fundy tides used for tidal energy?

6. Write a story about the tides of Fundy. Either write about "The Day the Tide Came in - Too Far!" or "A Most Unusual Find After the Tide Went Out".

CANADA'S CAPITAL CITIES

Québec City, the Capital of Québec

Québec City, the cradle of French civilization in North America, is the only walled city north of Mexico. Québec City lies at the point where the St. Charles River flows into the St. Lawrence River. It is the oldest city in Canada.

In 1608, Samuel de Champlain, a French explorer, established a permanent settlement there. In 1620, he built Fort St. Louis on the site where the Château Frontenac, a castlelike hotel, now stands. The French colony prospered in the 1600's, becoming the centre of New France and enjoying a brisk trade with its mother country, which was at peace with its rival, England, from 1632 to 1688. This tranquility ended in 1690 with a British attack on the city. Québec was successfully defended for sixty years due to its natural defenses as well as the protective wall and fortifications built around Upper Town in 1720. In 1759, however, Québec fell to Britain. On September 13, British General James Wolfe and his troops scaled the sheer cliffs to reach the Plains of Abraham, known today as Battlefield Park. They surprised and defeated the Marquis de Montcalm and his troops in about twenty minutes. With the Treaty of Paris in 1763, France lost the province to Great Britain. The French city became British but in name only; in spirit, culture and tradition, Québec remained French. In 1775, American troops led by Generals Richard Montgomery and Benedict Arnold were defeated. Upper and Lower Canada (the present day provinces of Ontario and Québec) were formed in 1791. Québec City became the capital of Lower Canada at that time.

During the last years of the eighteenth century and most of the nineteenth century, Québec was a shipbuilding and wheat-and-lumber-trading centre. City walls and other defenses were refortified. By 1880, most English speaking settlers had moved to Montréal, the United States or elsewhere leaving Québec the predominantly French city it is today.

Today Québec is a beautiful city decorated in grey field-stone with roofs of pastel shingles, stylistic steeples and impressive monuments. The city has been called the "Cradle of New France" because it served as the main base of early French explorers and missionaries in North America. Québec also has the nickname "Gibraltar of America" because of the Citadel, Québec's most famous landmark, a huge fort on the cliffs above the St. Lawrence River.

CANADA'S CAPITAL CITIES

Québec covers 93 square km (36 sq. miles). It has an old section that makes up 10 sq. km (4 sq. mi). This old section has two parts:

1. **Lower Town** squeezes in between the river and a steep cliff and includes the business and industrial districts of Québec; it has possibly the narrowest street in North America (Sous-le-Cap), measuring only 2.69 metres (8 ft., 10 in.). A square called Place Royale is Lower Town's best known landmark.

2. **Upper Town** sits 61 metres (198 ft.) higher at the top of the cliff. Most of Québec's best hotels, luxury shops, monuments and parks are in Upper Town.

About ninety-eight percent of Québec's people were born in Canada. About ninety-five percent of the population have French ancestors. Most Québecers speak French, so signs and other public notices appear in that language. Many residents also communicate in English.

CANADA'S CAPITAL CITIES

Québec City Facts and Figures

1. Shade in the province of Québec on the map of Canada. Label Québec City, the capital.

2. Where is Québec situated?

3. What two nicknames does Québec have?

4. What French explorer established the permanent French colony in 1608?

5. Copy the following sentences and fill in the blanks with the appropriate words.

a) Québec is the only _____ city north of Mexico.
b) Québec is the _____ city in Canada.
c) The old section of Québec has two parts: _____ and _____
d) Québec has possibly the _____ street in North America.
e) Most Québecers speak the _____ language of their ancestors: today most are _____.

6. Draw and colour the flag and coat of arms for the province of Québec. Tell what each symbol represents.

7. What is the provincial motto?

8. What is the provincial flower?

9. What is the provincial bird?

CANADA'S CAPITAL CITIES

Québec - Landmarks

Québec enjoys the distinction of being the oldest walled city in North America. The citadel is built on top of Cap Diamant (Cape Diamond) - with a view of the battlefields. The citadel is part of fortifications built by the British in 1820. It took thirty years to complete the project. A number of interesting historic buildings can be explored inside the citadel. During the summer months the ceremonial changing of the guard attracts a large audience.

Below are listed other landmarks and special places to visit in Québec. Do some research and write a sentence or two telling why each place has some significance in Québec's history.

1. *Artillery Park National Historic Site*

2. *Le Château Frontenac*

3. *Museum of Civilization*

4. *National Battlefields Park*

5. *Place Royale*

6. *Hotel - Dieu Museum*

7. *Parliament Buildings*

8. *Québec Zoo*

Have you visited any of the above? If so, which is your favourite?

Can you recommend other attractions for people who are visiting Québec?

CANADA'S CAPITAL CITIES

Carnaval

The average January temperature in Québec is about -11⁰ C; usually there is a lot of snow in the winter. Québec's people are known for their playful sense of winter, making it a great deal of fun by skiing, skating, tobogganning, snowshoeing and ice fishing.

Québec's major event, Carnaval, is a ten day celebration of winter with the two metre (7 ft.) snowman Bonhomme as master of ceremonies. It begins the first Thursday in February and attracts visitors from all over Canada and the United States. Highlights of the event include parades, snow sculpture contests, ice-skating shows, races, games, fireworks displays, art shows, extravagant theme parties, an unforgettable canoe race across the St. Lawrence River and much more.

A) Design a poster to persuade people to come to Carnaval.

B) Invent and describe a new activity that would be fun to have at Carnaval.

C) Design and draw another character like Bonhomme for Carnaval.

D) Make a list of souvenirs that you would sell at Carnaval.

E) Pretend you are a reporter. Write a newscast for television or radio telling others about the activities at Carnaval.

F) Make a brochure to show people outside of Québec City what Carnaval is like.

CANADA'S CAPITAL CITIES

The Separatist Movement

Many French Canadians would like to see the province of Québec became a separate nation. These people, called separatists, claim that the provincial government lacks the power to solve their own problems and that the federal government lacks the desire to do so.

The city of Montréal about 240 km (150 miles) southwest of Québec City, is the headquarters of the separatist movement. Most separatists hope to gain independence for Québec by voter approval. Talk to your parents or other adults for their opinions. When you have gathered your information, write a report on your findings as well as your feelings about a sovereign Québec.

- How do you feel about Québec separating from the rest of Canada? Are you for it or against it?

- What would be the advantages to Québec if it were to become independent? What would be the disadvantages?

- Would a sovereign Québec have the economic benefits of a province?

- If Québec were independent, would the free trade deal be extended to it?

- What stand is the Prime Minister of Canada taking?

- What about Québec's Premier?

- Would Canadians continue to do business (trading etc.) with an independent Québec? Would the terms remain the same or would they change?

- What would Québec's relationship be with the United States? Would the United States continue to be interested in the Québec market?

- How do you think the next voting will be carried out?

Read current articles in newspapers and magazines to bring yourself up to date on this issue.

28 J1-33

Toronto, Capital of Ontario

Toronto is the capital city of the province of Ontario. It is now considered a mega-city due to the restructuring of its municipal government which was one of the most ambitious undertakings in North America. Seven large municipalities have been combined, municipal and provincial responsibilities have been revamped, and property tax reformed. Toronto is now divided into 44 wards. Each ward is represented by a city councillor. The new Toronto came into being on January 1, 1998.

Toronto is the 5th largest city in North America in population. There are 2.4 million people living in Toronto. Over 80 languages are spoken in the city and one third of Toronto residents speak at home a language other than English. Forty-eight per cent of Toronto's population are immigrants and by 2001, more than fifty per cent will be foreign-born residents.

Toronto is considered one of the best global cities for business and is home to 90 per cent of Canada's foreign banks. It has North America's third largest stock market exchange. Toronto has also been called "Hollywood North" by the film industry. It is Canada's number one tourist destination with 21 million visitors annually.

During the 1600's and 1700's North Americans used the Toronto area as a portage between Lake Ontario and Lake Huron. The first permanent English settlement at Toronto was established in 1793. Sir John Graves Simcoe, Lieutenant Governor of Upper Canada (the future Ontario), bought the land from the Mississauga Indians and called the capital "York", after the son of King George III, reigning King of England. In 1834, the town was named Toronto, a Native American term meaning "meeting place". In the same year, William Lyon Mackenzie King would carry on the family's tradition of politics, distinguishing himself as Canada's prime minister in the twenties, thirties and forties. In the late 1800's Toronto grew in importance as a railroad centre and as a centre of manufacturing. Toronto was also growing as a banking, financial and marketing centre. Timothy Eaton opened the T. Eaton and Company store which for many years was Toronto's largest department store. The energy of mighty Niagara Falls was harnessed to provide hydroelectric power. This guaranteed Toronto a cheap source of energy to run its rapidly expanding industries.

Torontonians enjoy each other's many different cultures and each June Toronto holds a festival of cultures called Caravan. Each culture offers unique ideas about how to live and how to have fun.

Torontonians also have fun watching the Blue Jays, their baseball team, or the Maple Leafs' hockey games or the Argonauts' football games or the Raptors' basketball games for recreation.

Toronto can boast of having the world's largest subterranean complex, an underground temperature-controlled pedestrian city stretching six blocks. Underground Toronto was begun in 1977 and completed ten years later. More than one thousand shops and restaurants, six major hotels and several entertainment centres lie along its long twisting passageways. Toronto's underground transit system is the second largest in North America.

Toronto - Facts and Figures

1. Shade in Ontario on the map. Label Toronto, the capital city.

2. Why is Toronto considered a mega-city?

3. What is the population of the city of Toronto?

4. How was Toronto restructured?

5. Write definitions for the following words:
   a) portage   e) immigrants
   b) distinguishing   f) distinct
   c) harnessed   g) cultures
   d) guaranteed   h) subterranean

6. What four professional sports teams are well established in Toronto?

7. Draw and colour the flag and coat of arms for the province of Ontario. Tell what the colours and symbols stand for.

8. What is the provincial motto?

9. What is the provincial flower?

10. What is the provincial bird?

Toronto's Landmarks

The CN (Canadian National) Tower, at 553.33 metres (1 815 ft.) is the world's highest free-standing structure. It carries a host of transmission facilities including FM radio, Toronto T.V. and microwave transmitting stations. The Tower opened in 1976 and almost immediately became one of the principal tourist attractions in the city, drawing an average of 1.7 million tourists every year. Elevators on the outside will take you up to the Sky Pod (in 58 seconds) to an observation deck and the world's largest revolving restaurant. Lots of stunt men have been drawn to the CN Tower: for example, one man rode a motorcycle up the 2 570 steps for a place in the Guiness Book of World Records. Another tumbled head over heels down the stairs in one hour and fifty-one minutes. Two people carried a 124 kilogram refrigerator (275 pounds) up the stairs in one hour and forty-seven seconds. For charity every year, participants compete for time when climbing 1 760 steps. The current record is eight minutes and seventeen seconds!

If you were a stunt man, I wonder what record you might be interested in breaking?

There are many other interesting Toronto landmarks and special places to visit. Research the following. Write a sentence or two telling the significance of each.

1. **The Sky Dome**
2. **Casa Loma**
3. **Art Gallery of Ontario**
4. **Ontario Science Centre**
5. **Old Fort York**
6. **Exhibition Park**
7. **Bata Shoe Museum**
8. **Canada's Sports Hall of Fame**
9. **City Hall**
10. **Black Creek Pioneer Village**
11. **The Canadian National Exhibition**

Have you been to any of these special places? Which was your favourite?

Can you recommend other places of interest for people to see should they visit Toronto?

CANADA'S CAPITAL CITIES

"Mega" City

In grammar, the superlative degree is the form of the adjective (or adverb) by which the highest or a very high degree of a quality is expressed, such as bravest, happiest, most amazing, most beautiful.

Use the superlatives listed on the next page in the sentences which describe many of the super features of this wonderful capital city. You may want to do some reading first, so that you may choose the best possible word.

1. Yonge Street is the _____ street in the world.

2. The CN Tower is the _____ building in the world.

3. Scadding Cabin, Exhibition Park, is the _____

   house in Toronto?

4. The Royal Ontario Museum, opened in 1933, has perhaps the

   _____ collection of ancient Chinese art to

   be found anywhere in the world, outside of China.

5. The Art Gallery of Ontario houses a collection of 15 000 works of fine

   art; however, the gallery's _____ fame rests upon

   its huge collection of sculptures.

6. The University of Toronto's Observatory contains the _____

   optical telescope in Canada.

7. Labelled as the _____ team in the National Basketball

   Association, Toronto Raptors Basketball Club began playing in

   November, 1995.

8. Toronto offers a wide range of theatrical productions as the

   _____ English-speaking theatre centre in the

   world, after New York and London, England.

9. Blessed with countless parks, Toronto is one of the country's

   _____ cities.

CANADA'S CAPITAL CITIES

10. In the heart of Toronto stands Casa Loma, a _____ medieval castle that looks like it might have been transported directly from a book of fairy tales.

11. Toronto is one of the _____ Canadian ports on the Great Lakes.

12. Metropolitan Toronto is one of the _____ growing areas on the North American continent.

Words to choose from:

busiest	largest	fastest	longest
finest	most wonderful	greatest	oldest
greenest	tallest	hungriest	third-largest

33   J1-33

CANADA'S CAPITAL CITIES

Toronto's Economy

Toronto is the chief manufacturing, financial, and transportation and communications centre in Canada.

Write a paragraph about each one. Use the questions below as a guide for your written report.

Manufacturing:
- What are some of the goods that are made in Toronto?
- About how many factories are there in the Toronto area?
- About how many people have manufacturing jobs?

Finance:
- What jobs are provided for people in the financial centres?
- Comment on the Toronto Stock Exchange.
- Why does Toronto provide many jobs for people such as stock brokers and bankers?

Transportation and Communications:

- *What is Canada's busiest airport?*

- *What railways serve the city of Toronto?*

- *How do people get around the city?*

- *When did the Toronto subway open?*

- *How do Torontonians deal with pollution from cars and factories?*

- *What are Toronto's highways like?*

- *What is the water traffic like?*

- *What jobs are available in communications?*

- *What are Toronto's daily newspapers?*

- *How many radio stations are there?*

- *How many television stations are there?*

CANADA'S CAPITAL CITIES

Winnipeg - Capital of Manitoba

Winnipeg is Manitoba's largest city as well as being the capital. It is located at the junction of the Red River and the Assiniboine River. It has a land area of 570 sq. km (221 sq. miles) and a population of about 616 800. Winnipeg lies midway between the Atlantic and Pacific Oceans making it the main transportation centre linking eastern and western Canada. The city is nicknamed "Gateway to the West" since it is the main distribution point for goods travelling west from eastern Canada. The name Winnipeg is derived from the Cree name for the lake 65 km (40 miles) to the north, win-nipi, possible meaning "murky water". Besides being an important transportation and business centre for prairie farmers, Winnipeg is also an industrial city with a number of factories where such things as farm machinery, aircraft, clothing, computers, etc, are made.

In 1870, under the leadership of Louis Riel, Manitoba joined Canada as a province. In 1873 Winnipeg became a city. In 1972, the thirteen communities which made up Winnipeg joined together as a Unicity. The government is comprised of a mayor and 29 councillors who hold office for three years. Who is currently the mayor of Winnipeg?

Winters in Winnipeg are cold. The average January temperature is about -19° C. B-r-r! Summers are short and warm. The average temperature in July is about 20° C. The yearly precipitation is 535.2 mm. The number of hours of sunshine per year is 2 230.

The people of Winnipeg have developed many means of entertainment. The city's ballet, opera and symphony are famous. The Royal Winnipeg Ballet is known as one of the world's finest ballet companies. Live actors perform at many Winnipeg theatres, including the outdoor Rainbow Stage. The city is famous for its male choir and other singing groups. The University of Manitoba and the University of Winnipeg are major centres of culture.

CANADA'S CAPITAL CITIES

Winnipeg - Facts and Figures

1. Shade in Manitoba on the map of Canada. Label Winnipeg, the capital city.

2. What is the population of Winnipeg?

3. What is the area of Winnipeg?

4. What are the two main rivers?

5. a) What is Winnipeg's nickname?

   b) Why is it so called?

6. The province of Manitoba, of which Winnipeg is the capital, is considered a prairie province along with Saskatchewan and Alberta. Wheat fields and grain elevators are familiar features on the landscape in the south-western part of the province. Draw the flag and coat of arms of Manitoba. Tell what the symbols represent.

7. What is the provincial flower?

8. What is the provincial bird?

CANADA'S CAPITAL CITIES

Winnipeg - Landmarks

On top of the grand Manitoba Legislative Building, the Golden Boy balances on one foot. The Golden Boy is a five ton statue sheathed in 23.5 karat gold that measures four metres (13.5 ft.) tall. He can be seen holding a torch in his right hand symbolizing the way to progress in the future. In his left arm he carries a sheaf of wheat which represents agriculture in Manitoba.

There are many other interesting landmarks and historic sites which reflect Winnipeg's rich and colourful past. Several are listed below. Do some research and write a sentence or two telling about the significance of:

1. *Grant's Old Mill*

2. *Museum of Man and Nature*

3. *Holy Trinity Ukrainian Orthodox Cathedral*

4. *Knox United Church*

5. *St. Boniface Cathedral*

6. *Le Musée de Saint - Boniface*

7. *Riel House National Historic Site*

8. *The University of Winnipeg*

9. *The Royal Canadian Mint*

Have you visited any of these special places? If so, which one is your favourite?

Can you name any other historic sites worth visiting in Winnipeg?

Winnipeg

Major League Sports

Winnipeg's football team was christened the Blue Bombers in 1935, the year they became the first western team to win the Grey Cup, defeating the Hamilton Tiger Cats 18 to 12. They went on to win again in 1938, 1941, 1958, 1959, 1961, 1962 and 1984.

A) What other teams belong to the Canadian Football League (C.F.L.)? They may not all be Canadian teams!

1. _____   6. _____

2. _____   7. _____

3. _____   8. _____

4. _____   9. _____

5. _____   10. _____

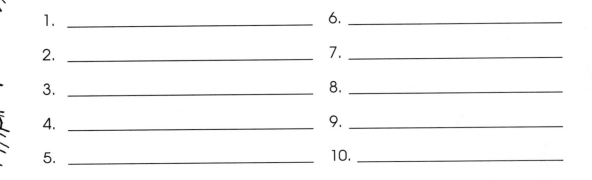

B) What is **your** favourite team?

Exciting National League (N. H. L.) action takes flight with the Winnipeg Jets hockey team. Originally they were a World Hockey Association (W.H.A.) franchise which brought instant credibility to the league by signing N.H.L. superstar Bobby Hull in their first year. They also pioneered the importation of European hockey players to North America.

Name at least four other Canadian teams that belong to the N.H.L.

What is **your** favourite team?

How are they doing <u>this</u> year?

C) Perhaps you collect football and/or hockey cards. If so, bring them to school and show them to your classmates.

Perhaps you have "doubles" that you would want to trade!

Canadian Lakes

Lake Winnipeg with an area of about 24 341 square kilometres (9 398 square miles) is located in central Manitoba and is the sixth largest freshwater lake in Canada. English explorer Henry Kelsey may have been the first European to see the "murky water" (win-nipi) and adopted this Cree Indian name for the vast freshwater body. The lake soon became an important transport link between the Hudson Bay port of York Factory and the fur-trade hinterlands of the Red-Assiniboine watershed.

Do some research and find the names and areas of the ten largest freshwater lakes in Canada. Record the information in a chart like the one below.

Lakes	Area (km²) rounded to the nearest 100
1. _____	_____
2. _____	_____
3. _____	_____
4. _____	_____
5. _____	_____
6. **Lake Winnipeg**	**24 400 km²**
7. _____	_____
8. _____	_____
9. _____	_____
10. _____	_____

CANADA'S CAPITAL CITIES

Regina, Capital of Saskatchewan

Long ago Regina, the capital of Saskatchewan, was the home to Native North Americans. They roamed the grasslands hunting buffalo. They used the banks of the Wascana Creek for drying buffalo meat, and cleaning and stretching the hides. Thus the area became known as "Oskunah-kasas- take", a Cree word meaning "pile of bones".

In 1882, the Canadian Pacific Railway completed its trek across the plains of Western Canada and the settlement of Pile-of-Bones sprang up at the rail terminal on Wascana Creek.

Also in 1882, came a new name for the community - Regina, Latin word for *queen* to honour the British Queen, Victoria.

In the same year Regina was chosen as the capital of the Northwest Territories. At that time the Northwest Territories was a huge area of the west, including most of the prairies.

The North West Mounted Police (known today as the Royal Canadian Mounted Police) established their headquarters in Regina in 1882. Men and women come from all over Canada to Regina to train as Royal Canadian Mounted Police.

As the years passed many hard-working farm families arrived from Manitoba, Ontario, and the United States to work on the rich, treeless, wheat-growing land that was there. Many businesses began opening up also. By 1903, Regina was incorporated as a city with a population of about 3 000. In 1905, Saskatchewan became a province with Regina as its capital.

The city began to grow into an important trade and supply centre for the surrounding farms. By 1911, Regina's population was 30 000.

40   J1-33

CANADA'S CAPITAL CITIES

In 1912, a cyclone destroyed much of Regina; however, the city was quickly rebuilt.

During the 1930's, the Great Depression caused much of the world to be in a business slump. In Saskatchewan, the slump was especially bad because the 1930's were such dry years there; very little rain fell; crops would not grow.

Regina's economy was strengthened in the 1950's by the discovery of underground resources, mainly potash, used for fertilizer and petroleum. A steel mill and a cement plant were built. Thus the city's economy became less dependent on a good wheat crop each year. Regina's population went from 71 000 in 1951 to 139 000 in 1971.

During the 1960's three new buildings were erected, changing Regina's skyline. They were the sixteen storey Canadian Imperial Bank of Commerce, the sixteen storey Avard Tower and the thirteen storey Saskatchewan Power Building. In 1962, the Saskatchewan government became the first in Canada to introduce prepaid medical care for its people.

During the 1970's more construction took place. Among the buildings was City Hall, an ultramodern building where city government meets.

In the 1980's, Cornwall Centre, a huge shopping mall opened. Regina's population reached 162 613. Today it is 179 200.

Regina has come a long way from a "Pile of Bones" to the "Queen City of the Plains".

CANADA'S CAPITAL CITIES

Regina - Facts and Figures

1. Shade in the province of Saskatchewan on the map. Label Regina, the capital city.

2. Below are listed significant dates in Regina's History.

   In your own words, tell why each has some importance

   1882 - _____
   1882 - _____
   1882 - _____
   1882 - _____
   1903 - _____
   1905 - _____
   1912 - _____
   1930's - _____
   1950's - _____
   1960's - _____
   1970's - _____
   1980's - _____
   1990's - _____

3. Draw and colour the flag and coat of arms for the province of Saskatchewan. Tell what the symbols represent.

4. What is the provincial flower?

5. What is the provincial bird?

42

CANADA'S CAPITAL CITIES

Regina's Landmarks

The Saskatchewan Science Centre offers a playground filled with an endless variety of things to do and learn. The site is housed in the building that once functioned as Regina's powerhouse, hence the nickname "The Powerhouse of Discovery". A breathtaking prairie panorama greets you as you enter the building, with sky scenes and subterranean and underwater images. Inside, the Centre houses more than seventy permanent hands-on science exhibits, and hosts a variety of changing exhibits. Press a button on a bunsen burner to watch a hot-air balloon soar three storeys into the air; watch chicken embryos develop; or try out the Centre's ham radio station. Another feature is the one hundred and sixty seat Krame IMAX Theatre which uses a five-storey screen and a four-way sound system to present films in a giant form.

This is only one of the special places to see while in Regina. Listed below are several others. Do some research and in one or two sentences tell why each each one is worth visiting.

1. *Royal Saskatchewan Museum*

2. *Legislative Building*

3. *Royal Canadian Mounted Police Depot and Museum*

4. *Diefenbaker Homestead*

5. *Mackenzie Art Gallery*

6. *Saskatchewan Sports Hall of Fame*

Have you visited any of the above? If so, what were your impressions of them?

Can you recommend any other attractions to see in Regina?

CANADA'S CAPITAL CITIES

Regina's Wascana Park

Wascana Centre, surrounding manmade Wascana Lake is a unique 930 hectare (2 300 acre) park in the heart of Regina. The area includes parks and public buildings such as the Legislative Building, the Saskatchewan Centre of the Arts, the University of Regina, etc. It is truly a centre of government, cultural and education.

Birds love Wascana Waterfowl Park which features hundreds of water birds such as terns (birds that look like small sea gulls), coots (wading and swimming birds that look like chickens), grebes (diving birds something like loons), red-headed and yellow-headed blackbirds, and Canada geese. They feel so comfortable in the park that they refuse to fly south for the winter!

A Park Naturalist makes sure that the birds are healthy and safe.

- Pretend that you are a reporter for your school paper.

- Your assignment is to interview the Park Naturalist and ask him questions that will help you write an article describing his job.

- During your interview remember to use key words when asking questions: WHO, WHAT, WHERE, WHEN, WHY and HOW.

- Do some research on this interesting career so that your information will be accurate and enjoyable to the reader.

J1-33

CANADA'S CAPITAL CITIES

Growing and Harvesting Wheat

Wheat is the world's most important grain crop. Wheat seeds are ground into flour to make bread and other products. These products are the main food of hundreds of millions of people throughout the world. A good wheat crop depends on several factors.

- Do some research on growing and harvesting wheat in the province of Saskatchewan.

- Use the outline below to complete the research assignment.

a) **Climate and Soil**

b) **Crop Rotation**

c) **Preparing the Ground**

d) **Planting**

e) **Care During Growth**

f) **Effects of Weather**

g) **Harvesting Wheat**

h) **Enemies of Wheat**

i) **Amount Grown Each Year**

Canada's Capital Cities

Edmonton - Capital of Alberta

Edmonton, the capital of Alberta, has a land area of about 679 km² (262 sq. miles). It is located on the North Saskatchewan River which winds through Edmonton for 61 km (38 miles). It has a population of about 616 700, second to that of Calgary (710 700). Edmonton is farther north than any other large Canadian city. It is about 523 km (325 miles) north of the Canada - U.S. border.

In 1904, Edmonton became a city and in 1905, it became the capital of Alberta. A few years later it earned the nickname "Gateway to the North". Many miners, explorers and adventurers wanted to travel to the Yukon and the Northwest Territories. Edmonton became the place where bush pilots flew their supplies in small planes into the Canadian North. The location makes it a major distributing point for goods travelling to and from Alaska and northwestern Canada.

A festival known as Klondike Days is held each July to celebrate the Gold Rush days of the 1890's. How exciting it must have been in 1897 when gold was discovered in the Klondike - an area of the Yukon just east of the Alaskan border. Hundreds of gold seekers began streaming through Edmonton on their way north to the Yukon. It was the Klondike Gold Rush that first brought large numbers of people to Edmonton, which lies in the heart of one of Canada's richest farm regions. Many gold seekers saw rich farm lands and decided to settle in the area.

In 1947, an oil well not far from Edmonton began gushing out "black gold" - crude oil. Before long, hundreds of oil and natural gas wells dotted the rolling farm and ranch lands around Edmonton. Over the years oil and gas have brought Edmonton its greatest growth and wealth. Petroleum distributing and processing and the production of petroleum products are Edmonton's leading industries. Chemicals and gasoline are among the products made from petroleum. There are other goods produced in the city as well such as lumber and wood products, foods, beverages, clothing and fabricated metal products.

CANADA'S CAPITAL CITIES

Edmonton is also called "The Greenest City in Canada" by some people. It has more park land per person than any other Canadian city. Most of the parks border the North Saskatchewan River on both banks.

Edmontonians are proud of the Edmonton Eskimos football team, which won an unprecedented five consecutive Grey Cups (1978 to 1982). Peter Lougheed played for the team in 1949 and 1950 and then went on to become premier of Alberta. Edmontonians also love to cheer on their hockey team, the Edmonton Oilers, which captured the Stanley Cup in their fifth N.H.L. season. One of the greatest hockey players of all times, Wayne Gretzky, was a former player of the Edmonton Oilers.

In 1987, a tornado struck Edmonton, killing twenty-six people and injuring two hundred and fifty.

CANADA'S CAPITAL CITIES

Edmonton - Facts and Figures

1. Shade in the province of Alberta on the map of Canada. Label Edmonton, the capital city.

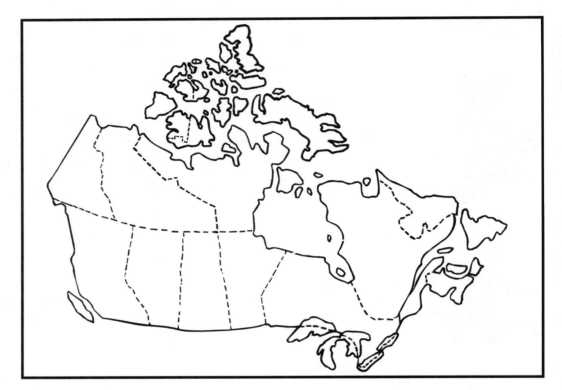

2. Edmonton has three nicknames. What are they?

3. What is the population of Edmonton?

4. What hockey great was a former player for the Edmonton Oilers?

5. What two sports teams make the fans of Edmonton proud?

6. Draw and colour the flag and coat of arms for the province of Alberta. Tell what each symbol represents.

7. What is Alberta's motto?

8. What is Alberta's bird?

9. What is Alberta's flower?

CANADA'S CAPITAL CITIES

Edmonton's Landmarks

The Provincial Legislative Building is one of Edmonton's most striking sights. Its reddish-brown clay dome is so well built that it has never shown one crack. Because of this famous dome, many people come from all over North America to study it and to try to learn why it is so strong. Alberta's provincial government leaders meet in the Legislative Building.

Listed below are other sights that are worth seeing in Edmonton. Write one or two sentences describing the significance of each.

1. *West Edmonton Mall and Fantasyland*

2. *Fort Edmonton Park*

3. *The Canadian Aviation Hall of Fame*

4. *1905 Street*

5. *Muttart Conservatory*

6. *Space Sciences Centre*

Have you visited any of these special places? Which one is your favourite? Why?

Can you add other special attractions in Edmonton to this list?

CANADA'S CAPITAL CITIES

Gold Fever

Edmonton is known as the "Festival City" for its array of celebrations. The famous Klondike Days is one festival that takes place annually in Edmonton.

A) The Klondike is an area of the Yukon. Discovery of gold on Klondike Creek led to the Klondike gold rush of the late 1890's. Do some research and write a paragraph about it. Using your information, write a poem describing that time in Canada's history. You may want to write it in the form of an acrostic poem.

K - _____

L - _____

O - _____

N - _____

D - _____

I - _____

K - _____

E - _____

B) Pretend that you were one of the prospectors who discovered gold in the 1890's. From your research describe how someone pans for gold. Write a sentence or two to describe the technique.

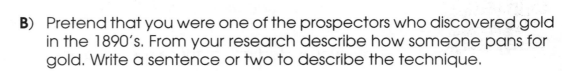

Tell how discovering gold would change your life. What would you do afterwards? How would you spend your new found wealth? Could there be any problems that might result from such a discovery? If so what might they be?

C) What is "fool's gold"?

50   J1-33

CANADA'S CAPITAL CITIES

Victoria - Capital of British Columbia

Victoria, perched on the southernmost tip of Vancouver Island, is the capital city of British Columbia. It is about one hundred km (62 miles) south of Vancouver.

In 1843, James Douglas explored the southern tip of Vancouver Island looking for a site to establish a Hudson's Bay Company fort. The site of Victoria was chosen as a fur trading headquarters. It was named after Queen Victoria of Great Britian, born May 24, 1819. By 1862, Victoria became a city and today it is Canada's most "British" city. Many tourists travel to Victoria looking for a bit of "Olde England". They ride in horse-drawn "tally- hos" or in London double-decker buses. They walk along streets that have British names such as Oxford and Balmoral. The narrow streets and gardens resemble those of England. Tourists shop for English products such as tweeds, teas and lavender, a shrub with pale purple flowers which when dried is used to perfume clothes and linens.

Tourism is Victoria's greatest source of wealth. About two million tourists visit Victoria annually. About one-third of Victoria's workers have jobs connected with tourism, for example, tour guides, hotel managers and restaurant workers. About one-fifth work for the federal, provincial or local government as clerks, secretaries, scientists, managers, planners, computer programmers, etc. Canada's chief naval base on the west coast at nearby Esquimalt Harbour was established in 1865. A number of people work in the fishing, logging, boatbuilding industries. Research and technology is a growing industry in Victoria. About one-fourth of Victoria's population is made up of retired people who live in Victoria not only for its scenic surroundings but also because Victoria has a milder climate than any other Canadian city, with temperatures averaging 16^0 C (60^0 F) in July and 4^0 C (40^0 F) in January.

Victoria was the proud host of the 1994 Commonwealth Games. Wonderful new facilities were constructed at that time at the University of Victoria campus. Local athletes as well as international competitors now take advantage of these facilities.

Victoria's Inner Harbour has always bustled with marine traffic bearing cargoes to faraway places, as well as visitors to Vancouver Island. In the early days, it was schooners and steamships. Today, the bustle is from passenger and vehicle ferries sailing between Victoria and Seattle, Bellingham and Port Angeles. There are also various float planes and helicopters flying between Vancouver, Seattle and Victoria.

CANADA'S CAPITAL CITIES

Greater Victoria (populaton 287 900) is made up of the city of Victoria (population 71 200) and the municipalities of Oak Bay, Saanich, View Royal and Esquimalt. It is Vancouver Island's largest metropolitan area.

Victoria is also known as Canada's "Best Bloomin' City". In spring the streets are lined with blooming trees and during the summer, baskets brimming with flowers are hung on the city's nineteenth century style street lamps. In February, while the rest of Canada is shivering through winter, local gardeners and flower enthusiasts join the "Flower Count" to tally the blossoms all over town. Four million blooms is not an unusual total!

J1-33

Victoria - Facts and Figures

1. Shade in British Columbia on the map of Canada. Label Victoria, the capital city.

2. Where is Victoria located?

3. Who was the city of Victoria named after?

4. In what year did Victoria become a city?

5. Why was Victoria originally chosen?

6. What is the modern role of Victoria today?

7. Why do many retired people move to Victoria to live?

8. a) What is Victoria's nickname?

   b) Why is it so called?

9. In what year did Victoria host the Commonwealth Games?

10. What is Victoria's population?

11. Draw and colour British Columbia's flag and coat of arms. What do the colours and symbols represent?

12. What is the provincial motto?

13. What is the provincial flower?

14. What is the provincial bird?

53   J1-33

CANADA'S CAPITAL CITIES

Victoria's Landmarks

Victoria is British Columbia's Queen of the Pacific. The domed buildings of the Provincial Legislature on the south side of the Inner Harbour look like a fairy tale palace at night when over 3 000 light bulbs outline the copper domes and stone walls. British Columbia's history and government are recorded within. Government leaders meet in the Legislative Buildings to make laws concerning schools, health care, mining, lumbering, farming and fishing in the province.

Other interesting places to see and visit in Victoria are listed below. Do some research and write one or two sentences telling why each is worth visiting.

1. *Victoria's Chinatown*

2. *Maritime Museum*

3. *Helmcken House*

4. *The Royal British Columbia Museum*

5. *Butchart Gardens (20 km N.W. of Victoria)*

6. *Government House*

7. *The Art Gallery of Greater Victoria*

8. *The Empress Hotel*

Have you visited any of these? If so, which was your favourite? Why? List other special places that people might enjoy visiting in or near your city.

CANADA'S CAPITAL CITIES

Totem Poles

The Pacific coast's Native people told many stories about the thunderbird. The mighty thunderbird made thunder by flapping its wings and made lightning by flashing its eyes. It speared whales and carried them to its home in the mountains. Thunderbirds were often carved on cedar totem poles. Today in Victoria's Thunderbird Park, people can see thunderbirds on many totem poles, where carvers create new totem poles in the Carvers' Shed and reproductions of ancient totems are on display.

The totem poles of Canada's west coast native peoples are unique. Not only are they spectacular to look at, they also describe important events and legends in the history of the families who owned them.

All totem poles are made up of carved figures or "crests" standing one on top of another. Animals are favourite subjects for crests because the west coast native peoples believed their ancestors spent part of their lives as supernatural animals.

Imagine you are a youth living in a village on the British Columbia coast towards the end of the last century. You are very excited because your father, a tribal chief, has just declared that a new totem pole will be carved and erected outside your home.

A) Number the following steps in order from one to seven to tell how that totem pole comes to be.

_____ Once the tree has been cut down, the trunk is hauled to the village where the carver strips the bark and outlines his designs in charcoal.

_____ Then the moment you have been waiting for – the pole is hauled up and propped firmly in the ground. You look at the totem pole's dramatic crests and feel a strong sense of pride.

_____ The time has arrived for the large gathering of family and friends to listen to the meaning of the new crests on the pole. Over many days there will be talking, singing, dancing and feasting. This is called Potlatch.

_____ Your father discusses your family ancestors with the carver about how the pole will look.

_____ After four months the totem pole is completed and ready to be erected. A deep hole is dug and lined with stones. Then a trench is dug from the hole to the base of the pole.

_____ The carver then heads into the forest in search of a perfect tree; red cedars are best because they are tall, straight and soft grained enough for easy carving.

_____ The carver's next task is to make the dyes for painting the pole. Burnt clam shells are used for white, red earth is used for a deep red colour, and for black he mixes mud, charcoal and salmon. Brushes are made by binding porcupine quills onto a stick.

B) Now design your own totem pole using wooden or styrofoam blocks, markers or paints, etc. Choose crests that represent something in your family history. Choose important events that you want to illustrate. Put it on display upon completion. Have fun designing your own family totem pole.

Canada's Capital Cities

Emily Carr

One of Canada's most famous painters, Emily Carr was born in Victoria, British Columbia in 1871. While still a child, Emily decided that someday she would be an artist. In 1890, she attended the California School of Design and later studied in London, England for four years. She then returned to Victoria and began venturing out to explore the remote coastal settlements that could only be reached by boat. The intense art of the ancient totem poles moved her deeply and she became interested in doing paintings of the totem poles.

She felt a kinship with the Native people and they accepted Emily easily into their homes and lives. They knew that she respected them and their way of life. In one visit to a small community, the natives gave her a new name "Klee Wyck" which meant "Laughing One".

In 1910, Emily went to Paris to study "the new art". Later she returned to Vancouver and exhibited her European work. She received no encouragement and returned to Victoria where for the next fifteen years she turned her creative talents to writing books.

In 1927, at the age of fifty-six, Emily met the eastern Canadian painters of the Group of Seven. Their work impressed her and she was inspired to begin painting again, this time concentrating on the forest landscape. For the last eighteen years of her life, Emily Carr brought the images of energy and life that she found in the wild into hundreds of drawings and canvases.

Follow-up:

1. Write a paragraph that Emily Carr might have written to describe the hardships and triumphs of being a female artist in nineteenth-century Canada.

2. Close your eyes and imagine a beautiful woodland scene. Make a list of your most vivid images. Use this list to paint a picture. Put your finished product on display in the classroom.

3. Research other well-known Canadian artists associated with a particular area of Canada. Write a report on your chosen artist and share it with your classmates.

4. Get a "feel" for your environment. Take outside a sheet of strong paper and wax crayons of various colours. Lay the paper on surfaces with interesting textures such as tree bark, fallen leaves, rocky soil, etc. Rub the paper with crayon to reveal the texture, choosing expressive colours. Back in the classroom, write a poem about what you discovered or combine your rubbing with others to make a class mural.

From Coast to Coast

The Trans-Canada Highway was formally opened at Rogers Pass, British Columbia on July 30, 1962. Canadians could now drive, using ferry services on both coasts, from St. John's in Newfoundland to Victoria in British Columbia. Stretching almost 8 000 km (5 000 miles) the highway links Canada's ten provinces and is the longest national highway in the world. Motorists driving westward along the Trans Canada Highway travel through the Atlantic Provinces; Montréal, Ottawa, the Canadian capital; the upper Great Lakes region; the western prairie wheat fields; and the Rocky Mountains to Vancouver Island. What a trip!

A) <u>Trans</u> - is a prefix meaning across, over through or beyond.

e.g. Trans-Canada means extending from one end of Canada to another.

The words below begin with the prefix trans.

By reading the clues and using your dictionary, determine what the words are.

1. trans __ __ __ __ __ __ __ __   crossing the Atlantic Ocean

2. trans __ __ __   let through, send over

3. trans __ __ __   to hand over from one person to another

4. trans __ __ __ __   change from one language into another

5. trans __ __ __ __   change the usual order of letters or words

6. trans __ __ __ __ __   plant again in a different place

7. trans __ __ __ __   transfer from one ship, train, or car to another

8. trans __ __ __ __ __ __   across or beyond the Alps

9. trans __ __ __ __ __   a written or type-written copy

10. trans __ __ __ __ __ __   the carrying on of business

CANADA'S CAPITAL CITIES

Whitehorse, Capital of the Yukon Territory

The Yukon Territory took its name from the Native word "diuke-on", meaning "clear water". The Yukon occupies the territory in Canada's northwesternmost corner. It is bounded by the Beaufort Sea to the north, Alaska to the west, British Columbia to the south and the Northwest Territories to the east. The Yukon Territory is a vast unspoiled landscape of lofty mountains, lush valleys, and pristine waterways. About half of it is forested.

During the late 1800's gold was discovered in the Yukon. During the peak of the Gold Rush the Yukon became a federal territory, with Dawson City as its capital. During World War II, four decades after the Gold Rush, Canadian and American Army personnel building the Alaska Highway flocked to Whitehorse which became the capital city of the Yukon Territory in 1953.

Wrapped in mountains, covered in hiking trails and cut with the Yukon River, the Whitehorse area is rich in beauty. You might wonder how it came to be called Whitehorse. Back in the pre-Gold Rush era, there was not much in the area besides a treacherous stretch of the Yukon River. The steep canyon and rapids rendered it almost impassable to early travellers. So wild were the rapids they resembled the flowing name of a charging horse. The city has continued to be called Whitehorse.

Today Whitehorse has evolved into the transportation, communication and distribution centre of the Yukon. It has a population of about 18 000. Whitehorse became the territorial headquarters of the Royal Canadian Mounted Police which in 1995 celebrated one hundred years of service to the people and communities of the Yukon Territory. Each summer there are performances by the R.C.M.P. Musical Ride - a precision equestrian team of thirty-six horses and riders. Whitehorse is also the heart of territorial government and federal departments.

CANADA'S CAPITAL CITIES

Whitehorse - Facts and Figures

1. Shade in the Yukon Territory on the map of Canada. Label Whitehorse, the capital city.

2. What is the population of Whitehorse?

3. What is the Yukon Territory bounded by:

   a) to the north?
   b) to the west?
   c) to the south?
   d) to the east?

4. a) When did Whitehorse become the capital of the Yukon Territory?
   b) What capital city did it replace?
   c) Why did Whitehorse become the capital?

5. From the reading, write words that mean the same as the following.

   a) highest point
   b) ten years
   c) ancient
   d) developing
   e) of horse riding

6. Draw and colour the flag and coat of arms of the Yukon Territory. Tell what the symbols represent.

7. What is the flower of the Yukon Territory?

8. What is the bird of the Yukon Territory?

Whitehorse's Landmarks

The Whitehorse Fishway enables chinook salmon and other fish to bypass the Whitehorse Rapids Dam during their annual 3 000 km (1 875 mile) migration between the Bering Sea and their freshwater spawning grounds in southern Yukon. It is said to be the longest wooden fish ladder in the world. The Whitehorse Fishway includes underwater windows providing a closeup view of the migrating fish.

Do some research and write a sentence or two telling the significance of these other landmarks and special places in Whitehorse.

1. **The Robert Lowe Suspension Bridge**
2. **Marsh Lake Lock, 24 km (15 miles) south of Whitehorse**
3. **Lake Laberge**
4. **Yukon Gardens**
5. **MacBride Museum**
6. **Takhini Hot Springs**

Have you visited any of the above? If so, which was your favourite?

Can you recommend other attractions worth visiting in Whitehorse?

CANADA'S CAPITAL CITIES

Dog Sled Races

An annual event that takes place in February in Whitehorse is the Yukon Quest, a 1 600 km (1 000 mile) dog sled race between Whitehorse and Fairbanks, Alaska. Quest trails can be clouded in snowstorms, can have weather that is bitterly cold at -40° C, or can have ferocious winds that wear you down. However, mushers have come to know and love the quiet beauty of the trail during their 1 600 km endurance race.

Do some research on dog sled races and write an interesting report on your findings. In your report, answer questions such as the following:

1. What breed of dogs are used? Describe their appearance.
2. How are the dogs trained?
3. How many dogs make up a team for the races?
4. How are the teams hitched?
5. What do the dogs usually do during the summer months?
6. What types of sleds are used?
7. Where does the driver stand? What is he called?
8. What word does the driver shout to get the team started?

CANADA'S CAPITAL CITIES

Robert W. Service

One of the attractions in Whitehorse is Lake Laberge, the setting for Robert Service's ballad, "The Cremation of Sam McGee".

Robert W. Service was one of Canada's renowned poets. Though born in England in 1874, Service moved to Canada in 1894. He lived in the Yukon and worked as a banker. He wrote many ballads about the Klondike Gold Rush and the surrounding countryside. Two of his best-known ballads are "The Cremation of Sam McGee" and "The Shooting of Dan McGrew".

A ballad tells a dramatic story in poetic verse. Ballads are actually one of the oldest forms of poetry. Locate and read several of Robert Service's ballads. A ballad usually begins by telling about the characters and the problem or impending danger that the topic deals with. Usually the verses of a ballad can be set to music.

You try to write a ballad of your own. Your ballad can be about one of the topics listed below or one of your own choice.

1. *The Klondike Gold Rush*

2. *Construction of the Alaska Highway*

3. *The Whitehorse Rapids*

4. *White-water Rafting*

5. *Cabin Fever in the Yukon*

CANADA'S CAPITAL CITIES

The Royal Canadian Mounted Police

In the 1870's, settlers started to move overland into western Canada. The government set up the North West Mounted Police to bring law and order to these areas. Known as the Mounties they are respected internationally for their ability to solve crime and for their perseverance in getting their man! Their very presence holds many people in awe. Their uniforms are unique and quite striking to look at. Today they are known as the Royal Canadian Mounted Police and they are still the only keepers of the law in the Yukon Territory and the Northwest Territories. In 1995, they celebrated their one hundredth anniversary.

A) Read the following statements about the Royal Canadian Mounted Police (R.C.M.P.) and underline the correct answers. Consult reference books to verify your answers.

1. The North West Mounted Police was <u>first</u> organized in (1824, 1873, 1895).

2. The motto of this organization is (We get our man, Maintain the right, We work to win).

3. Those who apply to be a member of the R.C.M.P. must be at least (17 years old, 19 years old, 21 years old).

4. Recruits are trained in (Edmonton, Alberta; Whitehorse, Yukon Territory; Regina, Saskatchewan).

5. Graduates are considered (constables, corporals, sergeants).

6. The Royal Canadian Mounted Police was originally known as (The Northern Police Department, the Royal Northwesterners, the North West Mounted Police)

7. The name was changed to the Royal Canadian Mounted Police in (1905, 1910, 1935).

8. Women were accepted as recruits in (1968, 1974, 1980).

CANADA'S CAPITAL CITIES

B) When you think of an R.C.M.P. Officer, you may immediately think of a member in uniform driving a police car. However, the R.C.M.P. have a variety of responsibilities which are quite extensive and challenging. Several of these jobs are listed below. Read them carefully then decide which one would best suit you and write a paragraph explaining the reasons for your choice.

1. **Crime Detention Laboratory**: for example - a) hair analysis, b) document analysis, c) photography, d) finger-printing, e) ballistics (firearms)
2. **Identification Section**: members attend the scene of a crime, take finger prints, and gather information
3. **Undercover Drug Investigation**
4. **Police Dog Section**
5. **Police/Community Relations Office**

C) Draw and colour the traditional uniform for members of the Royal Canadian Mounted Police.

J1-33

CANADA'S CAPITAL CITIES

Yellowknife, Capital of the Northwest Territories

Yellowknife is located on the north shore of Great Slave Lake and lies less than 500 km (311 miles) from the Arctic Circle. It has a population of over 15 000. In 1967, Yellowknife became the Northwest Territories' capital. It is a major mining centre as well as the shopping, business, and government mecca of the Northwest Territories.

The city was named after the Yellowknife Dene who moved to the area during the early 1800's. In Dogrib, it is called "Somba Ke" which means "money place". Although the north Great Slave area was part of the fur trade era, it was not until gold was discovered in Yellowknife Bay, that the town started to grow.

In the 1930's, the gold discovery combined with the discovery of ore in the Great Bear Lake area and the widespread use of bush planes opened the area to prospectors. By 1936, Yellowknife was a boom town as men, mesmerized by the idea of striking it rich, poured into town.

Commercial gold production began in 1937, Con Mine, one of the two major gold mines within city limits today, began production that year, although it has changed hands several times. Gold production ceased during World War Two but a renewed demand for gold started after the war with the opening of Giant Yellowknife Mine, also still in operation today. Today the two gold mines remain major employers. Gold is mined as far as 1 939 metres (6 500 feet) beneath the city and is poured into bricks locally.

Many of the world's major mining companies are exploring for diamonds in the Yellowknife area. At least one company has developed a proposal to construct a diamond mine. In the future, Yellowknife could become the centre of the new Canadian diamond industry.

Yellowknife is surrounded by water. In addition to Geat Slave Lake, there are thousands of smaller lakes to dot the Precambrian Shield. The entire area is ideal for those who enjoy fishing, canoeing, boating, birdwatching, or just the exhilaration of being on open water.

The Northwest Territories Legislative Assembly Building which opened in 1993, was designed to accommodate the Northwest Territories' unique style of government. Instead of party politics, the Northwest Territories has a consensus government. This government based on aboriginal traditions is the only one of its kind in Canada. The aboriginal heritage of the Northwest Territories is also reflected in its seven official languages, which include French, English, Slavey, Gwich'in, Dogrib, Chipewyan and Cree. This territory is much smaller since the formation of the new territory called "Nunavut".

CANADA'S CAPITAL CITIES

Yellowknife - Facts and Figures

1. Shade in the Northwest Territories on the map of Canada. Label Yellowknife, the capital city.

2. Where is Yellowknife located?

3. a) What industry employs many workers in Yellowknife?
   b) What new industry may soon be developed?

4. There are seven official languages spoken in Yellowknife. What are they?

5. Write meanings for the following words:

   a) mecca
   b) mesmerized
   c) exhilaration
   d) consensus
   e) aborginal

6. Draw and colour the flag and coat of arms of the Northwest Territories. Tell what the symbols and colours represent.

7. What is the flower of the Northwest Territories?

8. What is the bird of the Northwest Territories?

CANADA'S CAPITAL CITIES

Yellowknife - Landmarks and Special Places

The Dene people of the MacKenzie District of Canada's Northwest Territories have occupied a vast area of land, covering about 1 165 500 km² (450 000 sq. miles) for the past 25 000 to 30 000 years. The Ndilo Cultural Village invites people to learn the Dene ways and traditions in a recreated family bush camp. At the village, elders can be seen engaged in such daily activities as tanning hides, crafting tools, or drying fish or caribou. Visitors to the village have the opportunity to try their hand at drumming, making a rattle, sharing Dene legends around a campfire and tasting traditional foods.

That sounds like a fun way to spend an afternoon!

Other special places to visit are listed below. Do some research and write a sentence or two telling why they are special attractions.

1. *Bush Pilot's Monument*
2. *Old Town*
3. *Wildcat Cafe*
4. *Prince of Wales Northern Heritage Centre*
5. *Northwest Territories Legislative Assembly*
6. *Northern Arts and Cultural Centre*

Have you visited any of these special places?

Do you have a favourite? Do you know of any other special places to visit in Yellowknife?

CANADA'S CAPITAL CITIES

The Ingraham Trail

The Ingraham trail is known as Yellowknife's playground. Named after Vic Ingraham, an adventurous traveller and businessman who helped build the city, this 70 km (44 miles) road winds through granite of the Precambrian Shield, home to some of the oldest rocks in the world. There are many small and medium sized lakes, great spots for fishing and birdwatching. This is Yellowknife's cottage country where city residents spend their summer evenings and weekends unwinding from the pressures of city life.

A) If you choose to fish in the lakes and rivers, major fish you could catch along the trail include the following. Do some research and write a sentence or two describing each one. You might include information on the size, colour, best time to fish, where found, etc.

1. **walleye (pickerel)**
2. **northern pike (jackfish)**
3. **lake trout**
4. **Arctic grayling**
5. **lake whitefish**

6. **round whitefish**
7. **lake cisco**
8. **burbot**
9. **suckers**
10. **yellow perch**

B) The Ingraham Trail Region is home to the Black Bear. Do some research and write a paragraph about the Black Bear. Include information about its appearance, size, habits, enemies, diet, where found, life span, etc.

Because of the possible dangers involved with the presence of the Black Bear when you are camping or hiking, it would be wise to write a list of safety tips in case you find yourself being visited by a bear at your camp.

Bear Safety Tips:

1. Dispose of garbage properly.
2. _____
3. _____
4. _____

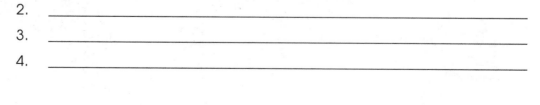

CANADA'S CAPITAL CITIES

Northern Lights

As the nights grow longer in Yellowknife, the green, red, pink and mauve lights of the Aurora Borealis, or Northern Lights, sweep mysteriously across the clear night sky. The aurora results from forms of electromagnetic energy which are drawn to the earth's poles, literally charging the atmosphere and causing it to glow. People come from halfway around the world to see this natural light show.

A) Look up the meaning of aurora in different dictionaries. Write the meanings. Find a meaning for the terms **_aurora borealis_** and **_aurora australis_**. Alter the definition to another form. For example, the meaning for aurora according to **_The Concise Oxford Dictionary_**, Fourth Edition, is **_aurora_** n. luminous atmospheric (Prob. electrical) phenomenon radiating from earth's northern (borealis) or southern (australis) magnetic pole, could be written as follows.

AURORA

luminous
atmospheric phenomenon
radiating
from the earth's magnetic poles

B) Experiment with various media to create effects like northern lights. Try crayon "engraving". Apply various colours of crayon heavily to manilla paper. Over these colours apply a black crayon. Produce the light effects by scratching off the dark layer.

C) Write a story in legend style about the origin of the northern lights.

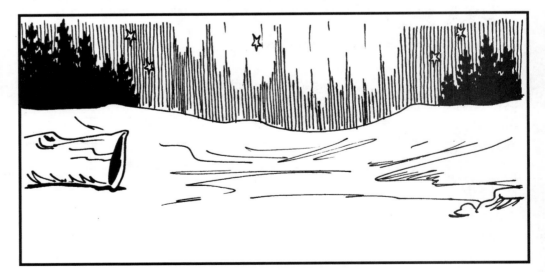

70   J1-33

The Mackenzie River

The Mackenzie River in the Northwest Territories is the longest river in Canada. It flows about 1 724 km (1 071 miles) from the Great Slave Lake (where Yellowknife is situated) to the Beaufort Sea. The Mackenzie River was named for the famous Canadian explorer, Sir Alexander Mackenzie. In North America, only the Mississippi - Missouri System is longer than the Mackenzie River System.

A) Find at least six other rivers in the world that are longer than the Mackenzie River. Tell where each is found (country or continent). Record the length of each.

B) Do some research and write an interesting fact about each river.

Example: The Amazon in South America carries more water than any other river and is the world's second longest river: only the Nile is longer.

CANADA'S CAPITAL CITIES

Ottawa - Canada's National Capital

Ottawa, the capital of Canada, lies along the south bank of the Ottawa River about 193 km (120 miles) west of Montréal. The mighty river and the city take their names from the Algonquian Indian tribe, the Odawa, who settled and traded furs in the area.

In 1613, Samuel de Champlain was the first European explorer in the Ottawa River region. Many settlers followed, developing a lumber industry along the river. After the war of 1812, British military engineers led by Lieutenant - Colonel John By built the Rideau Canal (1826 to 1832), creating a link to the St. Lawrence River that was safe from American invasion. Boaters and skaters now enjoy the 202 km long (123 mile) canal, one of the nineteenth century's greatest engineering feats. The frontier lumber settlement at the canal's end was named Bytown in the Colonel's honour. In 1857, Queen Victoria chose the town, now named Ottawa, as capital of the Province of Canada, later to be named the Dominion of Canada (1867).

At the centre of Ottawa is Parliament Hill, one of Canada's most popular tourist attractions. Parliament Hill is comprised of three buildings: the Centre Block, the East Block and the West Block all standing on a cliff overlooking the Ottawa River. The fire of 1916 destroyed most of the Centre Block. The Senate and the House of Commons in the Centre Block work to shape the laws of Canada. The Library of Parliament, attached to the Centre Block, miraculously escaped the 1916 fire. The great central tower of the Centre Block - the Peace Tower - houses a fifty three - bell carillon, a huge clock, and the Memorial Chamber commemorating Canada's war dead. The Traditional Changing-of-the-Guard ceremony takes place in front of the Peace Tower.

The East Block, completed in 1865, is the oldest of the three buildings on the Hill. Here are the historic offices – Privy Council Chamber where Cabinet meet, the Governor General's office and the offices of two Fathers of Confederation – Sir John A. MacDonald (Canada's first Prime Minister) and Sir Georges - Etienne Cartier. Canada's current Prime Minister, Jean Chrétien, has an office in the East Block.

The West Block contains offices for some members of Parliament and other government officials.

Ottawa has grown along with Canada and the federal government, Canada's Capital Region, including Metropolitan Ottawa, is now the fourth largest metropolitan area in Canada with a population of over 920 000.

CANADA'S CAPITAL CITIES

The Canadian Tulip Festival is one of the major events celebrated in Ottawa. Millions of tulips carpet the Capital in a brilliant display each spring. A huge gift of 10 000 tulip bulbs comes every year from the Netherlands' government in recognition of the refuge granted to the Dutch Royal Family during World War Two. This international friendship has continued since then. At about the same time, there is the colourful Tulip Flotilla, a giant parade of decorated boats on the Rideau Canal. In winter, North America's most famous winter festival, Winterlude, is celebrated. This spectacular winter carnival with dozens of outdoor events is centred on the world's longest skating rink - the historic Rideau Canal.

Ottawa can also boast about its professional sports teams - the Ottawa Lynx, Triple - A baseball team; the Ottawa Rough Riders football team; and the Ottawa Senators National Hockey team.

CANADA'S CAPITAL CITIES

Ottawa - Facts and Figures

1. Shade in the province of Ontario on the map. Label Ottawa, the national capital.

2. Who was the first European explorer in the Ottawa River region?

3. a) Who was responsible for the building of the Rideau Canal?
   b) When?
   c) How long is it?

4. In what year did Ottawa become the capital of the Dominion of Canada?

5. What three buildings make up the Parliament Buildings, Ottawa's most popular tourist attraction?

6. What happened in 1916 to destroy most of the Centre Block?

7. a) Write the following words in alphabetical order. They all begin with the letter **C** and have something to do with Canada's capital. Be careful.

   Canada, canal, clock, council, capital, century, chamber, cabinet, city, centre, commemorating, confederation, Champlain, commons, changing, current, colonel, central, ceremony, contains, carillon, completed

   b) Choose **six** words from the list and use each in a sentence containing an interesting fact about Ottawa.

8. What are **three** special events that enliven Ottawa?

9. Draw and colour Canada's flag and coat of arms. Tell what the colours and symbols represent.

10. What is our National Anthem?

11. What is our national motto?

12. What are our national symbols?

         J1-33

CANADA'S CAPITAL CITIES

Time Line - A Chronology of Events (1613 to 1967)

Arrange the historical events below in correct chronological order by writing the number of the event on the appropriate line on the next page. Use reference books to help you find the answers.

1. Construction of the Rideau Canal was completed.

2. The British government hired engineers under Lt. Col. John By to build the Rideau Canal.

3. Bytown became a city and adopted the name of Ottawa. Population was about 10 000.

4. Mayor James Ellis opened the new Carnegie Public Library with Andrew Carnegie in attendance.

5. On April 26, the Noon Day Gun was fired for the first time.

6. Samuel de Champlain, the first European to view the site of the future Ottawa, arrived at Rideau Falls, while conducting an expedition to search out a water route to China.

7. Ottawa was declared Capital of the Dominion of Canada. On July 1, Canada's first Dominion Day was celebrated.

8. The village of Bytown was incorporated with a population of about 1 000 persons.

9. Bytown was incorporated as a town.

10. Queen Victoria chose Ottawa to be the capital of the province of Canada. Construction began on the Parliament Buildings.

11. On August 29, the Windsor Hotel served the first meal in the world to be cooked entirely by electricity.

12. Ottawa's City Hall was destroyed by fire.

13. The Centre Block of the Parliament Buildings was destroyed by fire, but the Parliamentary Library was saved.

CANADA'S CAPITAL CITIES

14. The Great Fire of Hull - Ottawa destroyed many houses, leaving thousands of people homeless. Property loss was estimated at $100 million.

15. The city of Ottawa was granted a new Coat of Arms.

16. The new Canadian flag was raised for the first time on Parliament Hill.

17. Charlotte Whitton became the first woman to be elected mayor of Ottawa. The first Canadian Tulip Festival was held.

18. Canada's Centennial (100 year) celebration was marked by a huge party featuring a royal visit by Queen Elizabeth the Second.

1613	1824	1828	1832	1850	1855	1857	1867

1869	1892	1900	1906	1916	1931	1951	1954

1965	1967

J1-33

CANADA'S CAPITAL CITIES

Ottawa's Landmarks

The story of Canada's human history is told within the curved stone walls of one of the nation's newest museums - the Canadian Museum of Civilization. The museum was designed to resemble a moving glacier, reminding people of the powerful forces that shaped our land. The $255 million museum, which opened in 1989, is located across the river from Parliament Hill. The huge buildings sit on 2 000 concrete pilings to keep them from sinking into marshy ground.

Because the museum is so large, a West Coast native village, complete with war canoes and totem poles, was re-created, as well as a nineteenth century square and a shipyard. With its large - format IMAX movie theatre and special gallery for children, the museum draws 1.2 million visitors a year, making it Ottawa's most popular attraction.

Below are listed other special attractions in Ottawa. Write a sentence or two telling of their significance.

1. *National Gallery of Canada*

2. *Central Experimental Farm*

3. *Royal Canadian Mint*

4. *Supreme Court of Canada*

5. *Rideau Hall*

6. *Changing of the Guard*

7. *Peace Tower*

8. *Canadian Museum of Contemporary Photography*

9. *Canadian Museum of Nature*

10. *Château Laurier*

Have you visited any of the above attractions? Which ones? What is your favourite? Have you visited any other attractions?

77   J1-33

CANADA'S CAPITAL CITIES

Name the Prime Minister

Ottawa is the home of the Prime Minister of Canada.

Study the chart on the Prime Ministers and then answer the questions that follow.

Prime Ministers	When They Were Born	When They Served	Age When Sworn In
Sir John A. Macdonald	Jan. 11, 1815	1867 - 1873	52 years
Alexander Mackenzie	Jan. 28, 1822	1873 - 1878	51 years
Sir John A. Macdonald	Jan. 11, 1815	1876 - 1891	63 years
Sir John J. C. Abbott	Mar. 12, 1821	1891 - 1892	70 years
Sir John S. D. Thompson	Nov. 10, 1844	1892 - 1894	48 years
Sir Mackenzie Bowell	Dec. 27, 1823	1894 - 1896	70 years
Sir Charles Tupper	July 2, 1821	1896	74 years
Sir Wilfred Laurier	Nov. 20, 1841	1896 - 1911	54 years
Sir Robert L. Borden	June 26, 1854	1911 - 1917	57 years
Sir Robert L. Borden	June 26, 1854	1917 - 1920	63 years
Arthur Melghen	June 16, 1874	1920 - 1921	46 years
W. L. Mackenzie King	Dec. 17, 1874	1921 - 1926	47 years
Arthur Melghen	June 16, 1874	1926	52 years
W. L. Mackenzie King	Dec. 17, 1874	1926 - 1930	51 years
Richard B. Bennett	July 3, 1870	1930 - 1935	60 years
W. L. Mackenzie King	Dec. 17, 1874	1935 - 1948	60 years
Louis S. St. Laurent	Feb. 1, 1882	1948 - 1957	66 years
John G. Diefenbaker	Sept. 18, 1895	1957 - 1963	61 years
Lester B. Pearson	April 23, 1897	1963 - 1968	65 years
Pierre E. Trudeau	Oct. 18, 1919	1968 - 1979	48 years
Joseph Clark	June 5, 1939	1979 - 1980	39 years
Pierre E. Trudeau	Oct. 18, 1919	1980 - 1984	60 years
John N. Turner	June 7, 1929	1984	55 years
Brian Mulroney	Mar. 20, 1939	1984 - 1993	45 years
Kim Campbell	Mar. 10, 1947	1993	46 years
Jean Chrétien	Jan. 11, 1934	1993 -	60 years

CANADA'S CAPITAL CITIES

Questions

1. Who was Canada's first Prime Minister?

   _____

2. Who is Canada's current Prime Minister?

   _____

3. Who was the youngest Prime Minister ever elected?

   _____

4. a) Which Prime Minister held office for the longest term?

   _____

   b) How many years was it?

   _____

5. In what year did Pierre Trudeau become Prime Minister?

   _____

6. Who was Prime Minister in 1967 when Canadians got their national flag?

   _____

7. Who succeeded Lester B. Pearson as Prime Minister?

   _____

8. Who was Prime Minister in the year <u>you</u> were born?

   _____

9. Who was Prime Minister during Canada's one hundredth anniversary?

   _____

10. a) Who has been Canada's only female Prime Minister to date?

    _____

    b) What year was she in office?

    _____

The Rideau Canal

The Rideau Canal, built between 1826 and 1832 is a linked system of navigable lakes, rivers and man-made channels, which runs 202 km (123 miles) between the Ottawa River and Lake Ontario at Kingston. A flight of eight locks rises more than 24 metres (nearly 80 feet) from the Ottawa River and marks the northern entrance of the canal. Lieutenant-Colonel John By of the British Royal Engineers was sent there to build a canal for military use in 1826, and he established his headquarters in the easily defended valley. The canal was never tested in war time. Today pleasure boats are the main users of the locks which are still operated manually as they were more than a century and a half ago. Today its stone bridges and enchanting lights add to Ottawa's beauty. In winter when it freezes over, the Rideau Canal is billed as the longest skating rink in the world.

People have built and used canals for thousands of years.

Do some research and answer the following questions about canals.

1. What is the purpose of a canal?

2. Describe how a ship moves through a canal lock.

3. Name the two most important canals in the world. Write one or two sentences to describe their importance.

         J1-33

CANADA'S CAPITAL CITIES

Capital Spell

A) Test your spelling skills as well as your Canada know-how. Correctly identify the capital cities that are descirbed in the sentences below.

Watch your spelling! Some research may be necessary.

1. It is the capital city of the largest of the Maritime Provinces.

   _____

2. The musical "Anne of Green Gables" is performed here each summer.

   _____

3. The provincial flag of this capital has a fleur-de-lis in each corner.

   _____

4. The training centre of the Royal Canadian Mounted Police is located here.

   _____

5. This is Canada's most northerly capital city.

   _____

6. This capital is spelled with an apostrophe and s ('s).

   _____

7. The area around this capital city is the most densely populated in all of Canada.

   _____

8. Pierre Berton, who worked as a television journalist and who wrote many books about Canada's history, was born in this city.

   _____

9. Wayne Gretzky led the Oilers to win three Stanley Cup titles in 1983, 1984 and 1987 in this capital city.

   _____

10. This capital city lies nearest the centre of Canada.

    _____

11. Canada's Peace Tower is housed in this capital.

    _____

12. This capital was the site for the G-7 Summit in June of 1995.

    _____

13. This city lies approximately 48⁰ north latitude and 123⁰ west longitude.

    _____

14. This capital city lies less than 500 km from the Arctic Circle.

    _____

CANADA'S CAPITAL CITIES

Iqaluit, Capital of Nunavut

On April 1, 1999, the Northwest Territories was officially divided in two with the creation of Nunavut, the first territory to enter the confederation of Canada since Newfoundland joined in 1949. The word Nunavut means "our land" in Inuktitut, the language of its aboriginal people, the Inuit, who represent 85 per cent of Nunavut's residents. Nunavut is a territory, but unlike the Northwest Territories, the word "territory" is not part of Nunavut's official name. Nunavut is the largest territory of Canada, covering 1 994 million square kilometres – one-fifth the size of Canada, which is 9.98 million square kilometres.

A plebiscite (public vote) to select Nunavut's capital was held on December 11, 1995. Iqaluit received 60 per cent of the votes, beating out Rankin Inlet. Iqaluit, which was called Frobisher Bay until 1987, is an Inuktitut word whose name means "place of fish". It is located on the shores of Frobisher Bay, on the southern end of Baffin Island in Canada's Eastern Arctic. The population was estimated at 4 556 on April 1, 1999. Iqaluit is the largest of 28 communities scattered over Nunavut. About two-thirds of Iqaluit's residents are Inuit, compared to other communities that are more than 90 per cent Inuit. The remaining one-third is a mix of cultures and languages, including a French population of about 500.

Iqaluit is the seat of the government, a central hub for transportation and communication, and a major centre for business and tourism. The Baffin regional hospital in Iqaluit is the only hospital found in Nunavut. There are five churches, four elementary schools, one high school and one college. There are five modern hotels, a handful of restaurants, and numerous shops. Iqaluit Airport offers state-of-the-art facilities and is a gateway to the eastern Arctic.

In July, the average temperature is 18°C (46°F) and residents of Iqaluit experience 20 hours of daylight ranging from weeks to months. In January, the average temperature is -25°C (-13°F) and residents have only 4.5 hours of daylight.

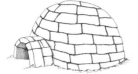

Modern Iqaluit blends ancient Inuit heritage and modern technology. Fifty years ago, Inuit lived in igloos. Today, the 28 communities of Nunavut are linked to the rest of the world by phone, radio and television. Many communities have access to the internet.

Congratulations to Iqaluit on becoming Canada's 14th capital!

Iqaluit - Facts and Figures

1. Shade in Nunavut on the map of Canada. Label Iqaluit, Nunavut's capital.

2. a) When did Nunavut officially become a territory?
    b) What is the language spoken by the aboriginal people, the Inuit?
    c) What does the word Nunavut mean?
    d) What is the area of Nunavut?

3. a) When did Iqaluit become the capital of Nunavut?
    b) What community lost the vote?

4. What is the population of Iqaluit?

5. Write three reasons why Iqaluit is an important community.

6. a) How many daylight hours do the people of Iqaluit receive in July?
    b) How many in January?

                   J1-33

7. The flag of Nunavut was officially unveiled on April 1, 1999. The colours, blue and gold, symbolize the riches of the land, sea and sky. Red is a reference to Canada. The inuksuk symbolizes the stone monuments built by the Inuit to guide the people on the land and mark sacred and other special places. The star, representing the North Star, forever remains unchanged.

Colour the flag of Nunavut.

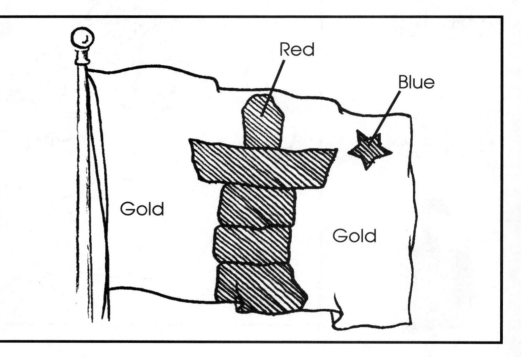

8. The arms of Nunavut were unveiled on April 1, 1999. The colours, blue and gold, symbolize the riches of the land, sea and sky.

The inuksuk (1) represents the stone monuments which guide the people on the land and mark sacred and other special places.

The quilliq (2), or Inuit stone lamp, represents light and the warmth of family and community.

The five gold circles (3) refer to the life-giving properties of the sun.

The star (4) represents the North Star which guides the travellers.

The igloo (5) represents the traditional life of the people and their means of survival.

CANADA'S CAPITAL CITIES

The Royal Crown (6) symbolizes public government for all the people of Nunavut and the equivalent status of Nunavut with the territories and provinces in Canadian Confederation.

The caribou (7) and narwhal (8) refer to land and sea animals which are part of the rich natural heritage of Nunavut and provide sustenance for people.

The compartment at the base is composed of land and sea and features three important species of Arctic wild flowers.

The motto, in Inuktitut – NUNAVUT SANGINIVUT – means "Nunavut, our strength".

Colour the arms of Nunavut.

CANADA'S CAPITAL CITIES

Nunatsiaq News

On December 11, 1995, after a sometimes bitter campaign between Iqaluit and Rankin Inlet, 60 per cent of the Nunavut voters cast ballots in favour of Iqaluit as the capital of Nunavut. The decade-old dispute over where to put Nunavut's capital was finally put to rest.

The following newspaper article was written for the Nunatsiaq News on December 12, 1995. Read the article carefully, then answer the questions.

Iqaluit Wins Capital Vote

Nunatsiaq News

IQALUIT -- It wasn't even close!

Analysts and capital campaign workers had predicted a nail-biter, but in the end Iqaluit took 60 per cent of the vote to 39 per cent for Rankin Inlet in the December 11 public vote for Nunavut's capital.

"We did it," said Lazarus Arreak, an Iqaluit campaign worker, moments after the results were broadcast over CBC radio on Tuesday afternoon.

Many Iqaluit supporters were surprised Iqaluit got almost 2 000 more votes than Rankin Inlet.

On Sunday, Rankin Inlet Mayor Keith Sharp predicted his community would win by a margin of 52 per cent to 48 per cent.

Although community-by-community vote counts will never be released, it appears that high voter turnout in the Baffin and low turnouts in the Keewaten and Kitikmeot made the difference.

Iqaluit Mayor Joe Kunuk says he was humbled by the support for Iqaluit, and he called on Nunavut's leaders to hold a meeting to promote unity.

CANADA'S CAPITAL CITIES

Nunatsiaq News

1. What is the headline of the article?

2. What is the name of the newspaper?

3. What were the residents voting for?

4. a) What places were competing in the election?

   b) Who won the election?

   c) By what per cent?

5. a) Who is Iqaluit's mayor?

   b) Who is Rankin Inlet's mayor?

6. What is Iqaluit's radio station?

7. Choose words from the article that mean the same as the following:

   a) promotion _____

   b) locality _____

   c) announced _____

   d) unpretentious _____

   e) foretold _____

   f) advocate _____

   g) edge _____

   h) togetherness _____

   i) examiners _____

   j) an assemblage of people _____

   k) followers _____

   l) set free _____

CANADA'S CAPITAL CITIES

Answer Keys

St. John's - Facts and Figures

1.

2. a) on the Avalon Peninsula at the southern end of the island of Newfoundland
   b) 83 sq. km (30 sq. miles)
3. a) Montréal
   b) Toronto, Montréal, Winnipeg, Edmonton, Calgary
   c) ninety-five thousand, seven hundred seventy (St. John's); one million, seventeen thousand, six hundred sixty-six (Montréal)
   d) St. John's - 96 000; Ottawa - 314 000; Halifax - 114 000; Winnipeg - 617 000; Toronto - 2 400 000; Regina - 179 000; Montréal - 1 018 000; Edmonton - 617 000; Québec City - 168 000; Calgary - 711 000

4. sheltered harbour; rich fishing waters
5. 1949
6. On the coat of arms, the white cross of St. George divides the shield into four parts. The two lions and two unicorns represent Newfoundland's ties to Great Britian. An elk is on top and figures of Native Americans are on either side. Blue section of the flag represents Newfoundland's ties to Great Britain; red and gold symbolize hope for the future.
7. Seek ye first the kingdom of God
8. pitcher plant
9. Atlantic Puffin

Halifax - Facts and Figures:

1.

2. a) 1749   b) Edward Cornwallis
3. a) Prince Edward was Halifax's commander and chief from 1794-1800.
   b) Prince Edward was very punctual and he expected everyone else to be on time also. When the Town Clock was built, it was placed where everyone could see it and it had four faces.
4. 114 500 (1991)
5. St. Mary's University, Dalhousie University, Mount St. Vincent University, N. S. College of Art and Design, Technical University of Nova Scotia.
6. a) Dartmouth
   b) the Angus L. Macdonald and the A. Murray Mac Kay

7. G - 7 Summit
8. On the coat of arms, the centre shield bears the blue cross of St. Andrew and a lion that represent Nova Scotia's ties with Scotland. Flanking the shield are a Native American, symbolizing the province's first inhabitants, and a unicorn, representing England. The flag bears the cross of St. Andrew and the lion of the Scottish kings.
9. One defends and the other conquers.
10. mayflower (trailing arbutus)
11. puffin

CANADA'S CAPITAL CITIES

The Halifax Explosion:

1. 1917
2. Mont Blanc; Imo
3. ammunition
4. Answers will vary
5. The explosion blew the Mont Blanc to pieces; levelled the north - end of the city; killed more than 2 000 people; injured 9 000 more; windows were shattered

Charlottetown - Facts and Figures:

1.

2.. a) Charlottetown Conference
   b) 1864
   c) Nova Scotia; New Brunswick; Prince Edward Island and Lower Canada (Now Ontario and Québec)
   d) Cradle of Confederation
3. Confederation Centre of the Arts and Province House
4. a) Atlantic Veterinary College
   b) Holland College Technical Institute
5. more than 15 000
6. The British named it after Queen Charlotte, wife of King George III.

7. The upper third of the Coat of Arms is a field of red on which there is a gold lion; the lower two thirds are white with one large oak symbolizing Canada and England and three oak saplings which stand for the three counties of Prince Edward Island. The provincial flag bears an adaptation of the Coat of Arms.
8. The small under the protection of the great.
9. lady slipper
10. blue jay

Fredericton - Facts and Figures:

1.

2. 132 km^2
3. 46 500 (1991)
4. the changing-of-the-guard ceremony
5. a) archives b) cathedral c) spectacle
   d) post-secondary e) internationally-renowned
   f) architecture g) academy h) observatory
   i) congenial j) fabrication
6. On the coat of arms, the crown symbolizes New Brunswick's ties with Canada. The lion represents the province's link with Great Britain; the galley stands for the early shipbuilding industry in the province; a salmon forms the crest; two white tailed deer support the shield.
7. Hope was restored.
8. purple violet
9. black-capped chickadee

 J1-33

Québec - Facts and Figures:

1.

2. Québec is located on the north shore of the St. Lawrence River where it meets the St. Charles River.
3. the "Cradle of New France" and the "Gibralter of America"
4. Samuel de Champlain
5. a) walled
   b) oldest
   c) Lower Town and Upper Town
   d) narrowest
   e) French; bilingual

6. The provincial coat of arms combines the emblems of France, Great Britain and Canada. The three "fleur-de-lis" are emblems of France; the British lion stands across the centre; the three maple leaves at the bottom symbolize Canada. The flag bears a "fleur-de-lis" in each corner. The white cross stands for the cross planted on Québec's soil by Jacques Cartier who reached the Gulf of St. Lawrence in 1534.
7. I remember
8. the Madonna Lily
9. the snowy owl

Toronto - Facts and Figures:

1.

2. Seven large municipalaities have been combined to make one huge city.
3. Population is 2.4 million.
4. Toronto now has 44 wards, one mayor, 44 councillors.
5. Answers may vary.
6. a) Blue Jays (baseball team), Maple Leafs (hockey team), Toronto Argonauts (football team), Toronto Raptors (basketball team).
7. On the coat of arms, the shield has the red and white cross of St. George, representing Ontario's ties with Great Britain. The three maple leaves symbolize Canada. The bear above the shield stands for strength.
8. Loyal she began, loyal she remains.
9. white trillium (also called white lily)
10. common loon

"Mega" City:

1. longest 2. tallest 3. oldest 4. finest 5. greatest 6. largest 7. hungriest 8. third-largest 9. greenest
10. most wonderful 11. busiest 12. fastest

Winnipeg's - Facts and Figures

1.

2. about 616 800
3. 570 km² (221 sq. miles)
4. Red River, Assiniboine River
5. a) gateway to the West
   b) It is the principal distribution point for goods travelling west from eastern Canada.
6. On the coat of arms, the buffalo symbolizes the importance of the Red River buffalo in Manitoba's history; the cross of St. George represents Manitoba's bond with Great Britain. The flag bears Manitoba's coat of arms and the British Union flag.
7. pasqueflower
8. grey owl

Major League Sports

A) Edmonton Eskimos; Toronto Argonauts; Ottawa Rough Riders; Saskatchewan Rough Riders; B.C. Lions; Calgary Stampeders; Baltimore Stallions; Shreveport Pirates; Hamilton Tiger-Cats; San Antonio Texans; Memphis Maddogs; Birmingham Barracudas

B) Toronto Maple Leafs; Montréal Canadians; Edmonton Oilers; Vancouver Canucks; Calgary Flames; Ottawa Senators

Canadian Lakes:

1. Lake Superior   84 500 km²
2. Lake Huron   63 500 km²
3. Great Bear Lake   31 400 km²
4. Great Slave Lake   28 400 km²
5. Lake Erie   25 800 km²
6. Lake Winnipeg   24 400 km²
7. Lake Ontario   19 300 km²
8. Lake Athabasca   7 900 km²
9. Reindeer Lake   6 600 km²
10. Lake Nettiling   5 500 km²

Regina - Facts and Figures

1.

2. 1882 - Community of Pile-of-Bones began when CPR went across the plains.
   1882 - Pile-of-Bones became known as Regina
   1882 - Regina became capital of the Northwest Territories.
   1883 - North West Mounted Police set up headquarters in Regina.
   1903 - Regina was incorporated as a city; population was 3 000.
   1905 - Saskatchewan became a province with Regina as its capital.
   1912 - A cyclone destroyed most of Regina; city was rebuilt.
   1930's - Little rain fell; crops could not grow.

1950's - A steel mill and cement plant were built; underground resources were discovered; economy was strengthened
1960's - Three tall buildings were erected; Saskatchewan offered free medical care to its people.
1970's - More construction - City Hall - where city government meets
1980's - Regina's population reached 162 613; Cornwall Centre opened.
1990's - Population - 179 200; known today as "Queen City of the Plains"

CANADA'S CAPITAL CITIES

3. On the coat of arms the lion symbolizes loyalty to the British crown and the three wheat sheaves represent agriculture. Red stands for prairie fires, green for grass and yellow for wheat fields. On the flag the green stripe represents Saskatchewan's forests. The gold stripe stands for the province's wheat fields. The flag also displays Saskatchewan's coat of arms and the provincial flower.
4. the prairie lily
5. the sharp-tailed grouse

Edmonton - Facts and Figures

1.

2. Gateway to the North, Festival City, The Greenest City in Canada
3. about 616 700
4. Wayne Gretzky
5. Edmonton Eskimos football team
   Edmonton Oilers hockey team
6. The cross of St. George represents Alberta's link with Great Britain. The mountains and foothills in the centre stand for the Canadian Rockies. The field of wheat at the bottom represents Alberta's chief agricultural crop.
7. strong and free
8. great horned owl
9. wild rose

Victoria Facts and Figures

1.

2. on the southernmost tip of Vancouver Island about 100 km (62 miles) south of Vancouver
3. Queen Victoria of England
4. 1862
5. a fur-trading headquarters for the Hudson's Bay Company
6. as a tourist, government, naval and retirement centre
7. scenic surroundings and milder climate than any other Canadian city
8. a) Best Bloomin' City
   b) In February, flower count totals around 4 million
9. 1994
10. about 71 200

11. Wavy blue lines represent the Pacific Ocean; the setting sun indicates that British Columbia is the most western province in Canada; the royal lion, the crown, and the Union Jack symbolize the province's link with Great Britain.
12. Splendour without diminishment
13. Pacific dogwood
14. Steller's jay

Totem Poles:
A: 3, 7, 6, 1, 5, 2, 4

From Coast to Coast:
1. transatlantic 2. transmit 3. transfer 4. translate
5. transpose 6. transplant 7. transport 8. transalpine
9. transcript 10. transaction

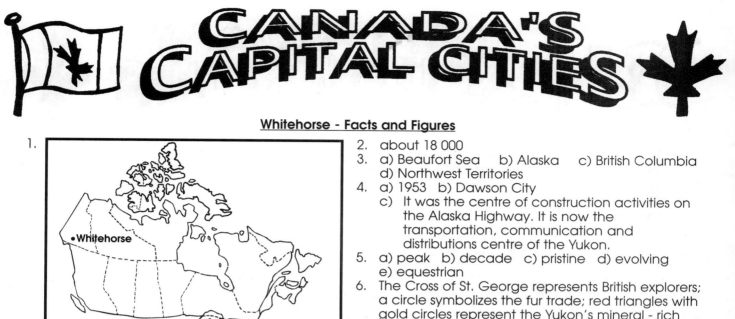

CANADA'S CAPITAL CITIES

Whitehorse - Facts and Figures

1.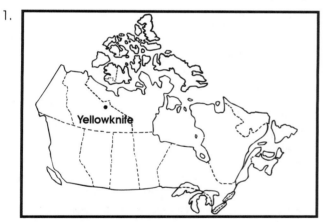

2. about 18 000
3. a) Beaufort Sea   b) Alaska   c) British Columbia
   d) Northwest Territories
4. a) 1953   b) Dawson City
   c) It was the centre of construction activities on
   the Alaska Highway. It is now the
   transportation, communication and
   distributions centre of the Yukon.
5. a) peak   b) decade   c) pristine   d) evolving
   e) equestrian
6. The Cross of St. George represents British explorers;
   a circle symbolizes the fur trade; red triangles with
   gold circles represent the Yukon's mineral - rich
   mountains; wavy stripes represent its river.
7. fireweed
8. raven

The Royal Canadian Police:

A) 1. 1873   2. Maintain the Right   3. 19 years old   4. Regina, Saskatchewan   5. constables
   6. The North West Mounted Police   7. 1905   8. 1974

Yellowknife - Facts and Figures

1.

2. in the Northwest Territories on the north shore of
   Great Slave Lake; it lies less than 500 km (311
   miles) from the Arctic Circle
3. a) gold mines   b) diamond mining
4. French, English, Slavey, Gwich'in, Dogrib,
   Chipewyan, Cree
5. Answers will vary according to dictionary used.
6. A wavy blue line represents the Northwest
   Passage; gold bars symbolize mineral wealth; a
   white fox symbolizes the fur industry and two
   narwhals (Arctic whales) guard a compass rose,
   which symbolizes the magnetic North Pole
7. mountain avens
8. gyrfalcon

Ottawa - Facts and Figures

1.

2. Samuel de Champlain
3. a) Col. John By b) 1826 - 1832 c) 202 km (123 miles)
4. 1867
5. Centre Block, East Block, West Block
6. Fire
7. a) cabinet, Canada, canal, capital, carillon,
   central, centre, century, ceremony,
   chamber, Champlain, changing, city, clock,
   colonel, commemorating, commons,
   completed, confederation, contains,
   council, current
   b) Answers will vary.

93   J1-33

8. Canadian Tulip Festival, Tulip Flotilla, Winterlude
9. The national flag has red and white stripes with a red maple leaf in the centre. The Coat of Arms has three maple leaves below the royal arms of England, Scotland, Ireland and France.
10. "O Canada"
11. from sea to sea
12. maple leaf and beaver

Time Line - A Chronology of Events (1613-1967):

6 (1613); 2 (1824); 8 (1828); 1 (1832); 9 (1850); 3 (1855); 10 (1857); 7 (1867); 5 (1869); 11 (1892); 14 (1900); 4 (1900); 13 (1916); 12 (1931); 17 (1951); 15 (1954); 16 (1965); 18 (1967)

Name the Prime Minister:

1. Sir John A. MacDonald 2. Jean Chrétien 3. Joseph Clarke 4. a) W.L. Mackenzie King b) 22 years
5. 1968 6. Lester B. Pearson 7. Pierre Trudeau 8. Answers will vary. 9. Lester B. Pearson
10. a) Kim Campbell b) 1993

Canada's Capital Spell:

1. Fredericton 2. Charlottetown 3. Québec 4. Regina 5. Iqaluit 6. St. John's 7. Toronto
8. Whitehorse 9. Edmonton 10. Winnipeg 11. Ottawa 12. Halifax 13. Victoria

Iqaluit - Facts and Figures

1.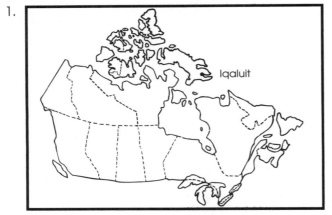

2. a) April 1, 1999
   b) Inuktitut
   c) "our land"
   d) 1 994 million square kilometres
3. a) December 11, 1995
   b) Rankin Inlet
4. 4 556 (1999)
5. Possible Answers:
   • Iqaluit has the only hospital in Nunavut.
   • Iqaluit has an airport.
   • Iqaluit has churches, schools and a college.
   • Iqaluit is the seat of government.
   • Iqaluit is a central hub for transportation and communication.
   • Iqaluit is a major centre for business and tourism.

6. a) 20 hours of daylight
   b) 4.5 hours of daylight

Nunatsiaq News

1. Iqaluit Wins Capital Vote
2. Nunatsiaq News
3. Nunavut's capital
4. a) Iqaluit and Rankin Inlet
   b) Iqaluit
   c) 60 per cent
5. a) Joe Kunuk
   b) Keith Sharp
6. CBC Radio

7. a) campaign
   b) community
   c) broadcast
   d) humbled
   e) predicted
   f) promote
   g) margin
   h) unit
   i) analysts
   j) turnout
   k) supporters
   l) released